MW00477161

Gerrymandering

Praise for

Gerrymandering: A Guide to Congressional Redistricting,
Dark Money, and the US Supreme Court

"Franklin L. Kury's excellent book is as trenchant as it is timely. In it, he provides a great overview of the redistricting process in states like Pennsylvania. He shows how utterly broken that process is in that state and how gerrymandering in places like Pennsylvania is so clearly at odds with the fundamental values that ought to undergird republican democracies. He also shows why it is high time we did something about it." —**Tom Wolf**, Governor of Pennsylvania

"If you care about building an inclusive democracy, that lifts all people's voices, then Kury's book is a must-read. It presents the real life drama of gerrymandering that is more spellbinding than any spy novel. And it gives practical guidance for activists that is easier to follow than an IKEA manual. Bravo!" —**Kathay Feng**, executive director, California Common Cause; National Redistricting Director, Common Cause

"Kury has captured the essence of the political blood sport of gerrymandering. He has taken a wonky issue down to the brass tacks of its political gamesmanship. Voters must choose their representatives rather than politicians choosing their voters." —**Pamela Goodman**, president of the League of Women Voters of Florida

"Gerrymandering for partisan gain, an issue few citizens understand, threatens our democracy. Franklin L. Kury, in this easy-to-read masterpiece, explains how Pennsylvania's redistricting has infringed on the rights of millions of Pennsylvania's voters whose voices are muted by the current gerrymandering. His remedy is simple: citizens must become engaged and—through legal action, intense lobbying, and the power of the purse—must force their legislators to devise fair representation." —**Shirley Anne Warshaw**, chair, Harold G. Evans Eisenhower Leadership Studies, Gettysburg College

"Kury's concise and well-documented primer on gerrymandering should be of interest to legislators who draw the lines, journalists who write about the process, teachers and students who want to understand it, and perhaps most importantly to citizens who will find in his Citizen's Toolbox ideas for how to improve the way we are represented by our lawmakers in our nation's Capital." —**Joseph P. McLaughlin Jr.**, director, Temple University Institute for Public Affairs

"Franklin L. Kury shines light on how political parties gain and hold onto power—even when they lose the majority support of their constituents. He breaks down the inherent conflict of elected officials being allowed to pick their voters and the dark money enabling them. Fortunately for us, Kury isn't content to just report from the sidelines. His guide shows how states like California are leading the way to reform and provides specific steps you can take to bring fair electoral districts to your state." —**Christina Shupe**, director, California Citizens Redistricting Commission

[handwritten inscription: Dec 5, 2018 — For Margaret ... McCormick, with best wishes + ... regards for your career of ...]

Gerrymandering

A Guide to Congressional Redistricting, Dark Money, and the US Supreme Court

Franklin L. Kury

Hamilton Books
an imprint of
ROWMAN & LITTLEFIELD
Lanham • Boulder • New York • London

Copyright © 2018 by
The Rowman & Littlefield Publishing Group, Inc.
4501 Forbes Boulevard
Suite 200
Lanham, Maryland 20706
Hamilton Acquisitions Department (301) 459-3366

Unit A, Whitacre Mews, 26-34 Stannary Street,
London SE11 4AB, United Kingdom

All rights reserved
Printed in the United States of America
British Library Cataloging in Publication Information Available

Library of Congress Control Number:
Library of Congress Control Number: 2018939531

∞™ The paper used in this publication meets the minimum
requirements of American National Standard for Information
Sciences—Permanence of Paper for Printed Library Materials,
ANSI Z39.48-1992

Printed in the United States of America

For Barney and Helen Kury, my parents, the children of Polish immigrants, who raised their children to believe that participation in politics is an essential part of life.

ALSO BY FRANKLIN L. KURY

Clean Politics, Clean Streams
A Legislative Autobiography and Reflections
(2011)

Why Are You Here?
A Primer for State Legislators and Citizens
(2014)

Contents

List of Figures

Introduction

Imagine a National Football League (NFL) game between the New England Patriots and the Dallas Cowboys. The Patriots win and then they—the Patriots, not the NFL—announce new rules for future games. The Cowboys will have to gain 150 yards to score a touchdown, but the Patriots will only need to do 50 yards. Outrageous? Of course, and the fans would scream in protest. Keep this hypothetical football game in the back of your mind as you read on. It illustrates the basic question this book addresses. Who sets the rules for the competing teams in our elections for the US House of Representatives, and how is it done?

The nub of the matter is this. We have a representative form of government. We do not directly vote on legislation, in either Washington or our state capitals. We elect someone to speak for us in the legislative halls. Elected representatives should speak and act in a manner that validly reflects the opinion of the voters who elect them. Without that, the system fails.

The US House of Representatives was designed by James Madison and the other Constitution writers to represent the populations of the states. The Constitution places power in the hands of the House (along with the Senate) to deal with taxes, war and military affairs, immigration, interstate commerce, and other subjects with great impact on our lives. In other words, the rules that govern the elections to the US House really determine who will exercise the immense power of the Congress.

Figure 0.1. 115th Congressional District map. It shows the changes in the number of congressional seats in each state after the 2010 census. A new redistricting will take place after the 2020 census (photo: Wikimedia Commons).

The entire population of the United States, which was 323.1 million in 2016, is represented in the US House by 435 representatives. The US population is so large that the people are placed in 435 congressional districts, and each elects one congressperson.

Pennsylvania, with a 2016 population of 12.7 million, has eighteen congressional districts. California, with a 2016 population of 39.25 million, has fifty-three congressional districts. Under the "one person, one vote" rule (to be discussed later), each district is mandated to contain about 705,000.

The number of representatives from each state is determined by the US census taken every ten years. Some states, like California and Arizona, are robustly growing in population so they get more congressional seats after each census. Other states, like Pennsylvania, are growing at a slower rate, so they lose seats in Congress.

Seven states, it must be noted, have only one US representative: Alaska, Delaware, Montana, North Dakota, South Dakota, Vermont, and Wyoming.

At one point, Pennsylvania had twenty-seven US representatives. In 2010 it had nineteen and now it has eighteen.

How many congressional seats Pennsylvania and all of the other states will have after 2020 will be determined by the US census of that year. The population of each state certified by the US Census Bureau is divided by the number of congressional districts allocated to that state.

This is where the hypothetical Patriots-Cowboys football game becomes relevant. Who determines how the population of a state is allocated into its congressional districts? And is it done to give one of the political parties an undue advantage in electing members of Congress? Is it done so that one of the political teams must go 150 yards to win while the other has only to go 50?

Throughout US history state legislatures have drawn the lines for their own district seats as well as the members of Congress in a system similar to the hypothetical Patriots-Cowboys game. This method of redistricting has been traditionally looked upon as politics as usual.

Those elected were often able to work with the other party, and the legislatures in the state capitols and US capitol functioned almost in spite of the redistricting rules.

With the redistricting following the 2010 census, the traditional map drawing has been radically changed. Computer technology and cash—unlimited cash—have put partisan redistricting on steroids and produced super-partisan gerrymandering of some state legislatures that in turn produce a US House of Representatives controlled by a block of representatives that has frozen the Congress in dysfunction. Locked in place by a band of ultraconservatives, the House has failed to act on serious issues such as the environment, tax reform, health care, infrastructure, gun violence, and immigration.

We, the public, are the losers in several ways.

Compromise became a dirty word, although it was an essential part of the legacy left to us by the writers of the US Constitution. Without compromise there would be no US Constitution, a document hammered together by men of strongly different views who placed the need for a new government above their own views.[1]

The legacy of compromise has been relegated to the wastebacket.[2] When President Reagan had to contend with a Democratic House, he and Speaker Tip O'Neill met for drinks and worked out a compromise. But when Republican Speaker John Boehner tried to negotiate with President Obama, the House Republicans forced him to resign. Even with the Republicans controlling both houses of Congress and the White House, the Congress is frozen in place.

We are all losers because our voices and opinions are largely ignored in congressional districts that are overwhelmingly rigged in favor of an incumbent who needs only to tend to his base in that district.

Contrary to the intent of the Constitution writers, the US House today does not truly represent the opinion of the American electorate. "The Republican House majority (elected in 2012) is impervious to the will of the electorate. Thanks in part to deft redistricting based on the 2010 Census, House Republicans may be protected from the vicissitudes of the voters for the next decade."[3]

This book explains how we got into this quagmire, and provides an understanding of what can be done to achieve reform and realistic advice on how to go about it.

At first blush, redistricting is a complicated subject beyond the comprehension of many. However, as Pamela Goodman, president of the League of Women Voters of Florida, told me, "At first, I found it murky, but after some study it became simple. The basics we need to know are not complicated."

This book seeks to enable readers to make this issue easy to understand and act upon. The book is intended for America's political "outsiders," citizens for whom voting is a serious responsibility, but politics is not the center of their lives. The book is based on the firm belief that the political power of the United States resides in its citizens, who temporarily grant it to those elected to public office under the state and US Constitutions.

The first step is to become familiar with the glossary that immediately follows this introduction. Many of the terms and phrases used in discussing redistricting have meanings somewhat different than their normal use.

Although the goal is to get a fair playing field in congressional elections, much of the book focuses on state legislatures for a fundamental reason—those who control state legislatures can control who goes to Congress.

This is a fundamental truth about congressional redistricting that the national Republican Party saw in 2010 when they snatched control of enough state legislatures to redraw the congressional boundary lines in their favor in 2012.[4] The Democrats were caught napping and did not realize what happened until it was too late.

This book recognizes that highly partisan redistricting is not the only cause of the congressional gridlock. The unlimited dark money authorized by the *Citizens United v. Federal Election Commission* case is just as important. But as the book shows, redistricting and dark money are intricately intertwined.

One should also recognize that both the Democratic and Republican Parties have done and will continue to do partisan redistricting when they can. But in the current redistricting cycle, the Republicans have been much better at it than the Democrats.

This book is not an argument to elect Democrats in place of Republicans, but asks instead for a fair playing field on which both parties have the same distance to cross the goal line.

As President Ronald Reagan declared in 1987, "a fair deal (in redistricting). And that's all we're asking for: an end to the antidemocratic and un-American practice of gerrymandering congressional districts."[5]

This book is not a partisan recital of criticisms of gerrymandering. It is intended to be a more balanced picture of redistricting that recognizes there are others who see it differently. Some of those differing voices are used in the text. (The dissent of Justice Felix Frankfurter in the *Baker v. Carr* case is an example.)

As explained, congressional redistricting is a matter that each of the fifty states must handle for itself. There is a wide variety of redistricting systems across the United States. Some states have already reformed their congressional redistricting system, and many have not. You will read how Pennsylvania and California are polar opposites in congressional redistricting.

Every reader is asked to review and critique the congressional redistricting system in his or her state. The information contained in the Citizen's Toolbox, at the end of the text, enables readers to do that.

In addition to describing the steps that can be taken to reform congressional redistricting, this book also relates the strong opposition that can be expected to block reform efforts by those who want to keep the US House of Representatives the way it is. Specifically, this is the dark money from the Koch brothers' network and others that can now be spent in unlimited amounts as "independent expenditures." Related to this is the difficulty citizens will have in trying to learn how much is spent on independent expenditures and the donors identified.

Chapter 1 is the anatomy of the redistricting in Pennsylvania in 2011. This chapter describes how it was done and shows the results as laid out on the maps of the state's congressional districts. Readers can use Pennsylvania as a measuring rod against which to compare their state.

Chapter 2 reviews the history of redistricting in the United States and tells how redistricting is done in a variety of ways, especially in those states that allow the public to enact laws independently of the legislatures by the ballot initiative process.

Chapter 3 reviews what can be done to enact a reform by a state legislature and what it takes to pass a ballot referendum in the twenty-two states that allow it. In both cases dark money is the adversary protected by a shroud of secrecy.

This chapter concludes with a shocking map and report that reveal how poorly independent spending is reported and disclosed in the fifty states. Judicial relief, as described in chapter 4, may be a better opportunity for reform, but that depends on what the Supreme Court of the United States does with the Wisconsin redistricting case that is expected to be decided in 2018. The plaintiffs in this case want their legislature redistricted on a new standard for measuring partisan redistricting, the "efficiency gap" standard.

Regardless of how the court rules, the work for reform advocates will still be a significant challenge. This chapter describes what the challenge will be if the court rejects the Wisconsin standard or upholds it.

The final chapter gives candid political advice on what to do in your state and how to go about getting it done. It invites you to undertake a significant civic challenge that will require a good deal of time and effort. It will be a grueling marathon, not a sprint. Following the text is a Citizen's Toolbox providing essential information, such as relevant constitutional provisions and websites for organizations that provide information specific to each of the fifty states.

There is a time deadline applicable to any action you may undertake to reform congressional redistricting in your state. The general election of 2020 is the effective deadline for action to reform congressional redistricting. On that date the state legislators will be elected who will draw the maps based on the US census taken the same year. The maps they draw in 2021 are likely to be in effect for the following decade, until there is a new census in 2030. Time, therefore, is of the essence in what change you seek.

There is one ingredient this book cannot provide, the enthusiastic desire to act. That must come from you, the reader. I hope this book provides fuel for your fire.

—FRANKLIN L. KURY
Harrisburg, Pennsylvania
December 1, 2017

NOTES

1. See Catherine Drinker Bowen, *Miracle at Philadelphia: The Story of the Constitutional Convention May to September 1787* (Boston: Little, Brown and Company, 1966).

2. See Jane Mayer's report of the Koch brothers' conclave when the participants overwhelming rejected Senator John Cornyn's openness to work with President Obama in favor of a hard no-compromise position argued by Senator James DeMint. Mayer, *Dark Money: The Hidden History of the Billionaires behind the Rise of the Radical Right* (New York: Anchor Books, 2016), 25–28. In Mayer's opinion, this was the moment when the die was cast for the US House of Representatives to total obstruction to President Obama for the last six years of his administration.

3. Dana Milbank, "Republican Gerrymandering Makes the Difference in the House," *Washington Post*, January 4, 2013.

4. See David Daley, *Ratf**ked: The True Story behind the Secret Plan to Steal America's Democracy* (New York: Liveright, 2016), xi–16.

5. "Speech to Republican Governors' Club Annual Dinner," October 15, 1987.

Glossary

Please study these definitions before reading the book. Understanding the terms in the context of this book is important.

Corporation: Not Campbell Soup or Ford Motor Company or another usual business organization. In the context of dark money, a nonprofit corporation classified as a social welfare organization in Sec. 501(c)(4) of the Internal Revenue Code. Contributions to these corporations are tax-exempt, and the donors' identities need not be disclosed.

Cracking: A tool used in gerrymandering that weakens the voting base of one party in a particular seat by spreading it out among several districts.

Dark money: Anonymous spending through independent expenditures to influence an election by organizations that do not disclose the identity of their donors. Under the US Supreme Court decision in the *Citizens United* case, there is no limit to the amount such groups can spend in elections so long as they are independent expenditures. *Dark Money* is also the title of a book by Jane Mayer that is an in-depth report on the subject.

Efficiency gap: A mathematical formula for showing excessive partnership in redistricting. The formula compares the statewide vote of each party with the share of seats that party elects in legislative elections. The vote shares for each party in each district are compared to show how many more votes were needed to win or lose in that district than was necessary for the outcome. These are "wasted votes," and the more wasted votes the greater the efficiency gap. "How the Efficiency Gap Works," in the Citizen's Toolbox, demonstrates it on a hypothetical model. The validity of this efficiency gap as a standard that shows a violation of the Equal Protection Clause of the Fourteenth Amendment is now before the US Supreme Court in the *Gill v. Whitford* case discussed in chapter 4.

Gerrymandering: Redistricting in a partisan manner so that the party doing the redistricting draws the district lines to maximize the political safety of its seats at the expense of the other party and the public at large.

Independent expenditure: Money spent to influence an election but not given as a contribution to a candidate or political party. If given to a candidate or party organization, federal and state campaign limits apply to the size of the donation. When spent independently of the candidate and party, there is no limit on the amount that may be spent.

Jurisdiction: Before a federal court can hear a case it must be authorized to do so by the US Constitution or a federal law. Without such authorization the court has no jurisdiction and must decline to hear the case.

Koch brothers: Charles and David Koch, ultrawealthy and ultraconservative businessmen who have astutely organized a network of similarly ultrawealthy and ultraconservative people to pool their money and spend it to influence elections, predominantly through independent expenditures.

"One person, one vote": A standard for measuring whether redistricting complies with the Equal Protection Clause of the Fourteenth Amendment to the US Constitution. It means that each district must have the same number of people. This standard has been the law since 1964. Computer software makes it easy to draw such districts.

Packing: Another tool used to gerrymander; this is cramming the voters of the other party into a single district to dissipate their strength in other districts.

Redistricting: Redrawing of legislative and congressional district boundary lines, mandated by the state and US Constitutions after each federal census. The term itself is neutral.

Chapter One

The Anatomy of a Redistricting—
Pennsylvania, a Gerrymander?

The plan to redraw Pennsylvania's congressional district lines to give the Republicans a larger share of the congressional seats began in late 2008, just after the election. The Democrats were elated. Barack Obama had defeated John McCain for the presidency, and the Democrats had been given control of both the US Senate and House of Representatives. The Republicans were depressed. What was their future?

Ed Gillespie, chairman of the Republican National Committee, and Chris Jankowski, director of the Republican State Leadership Committee, reviewed the national results and saw a way forward.

They noted that the Democrats' control of the legislatures in a number of states was thin. Michigan, North Carolina, Ohio, Pennsylvania, and Wisconsin looked particularly inviting. In Pennsylvania, for example, they saw that a change of two seats in the 2010 elections would give the GOP control of the state house and thereby the power to draw new congressional district lines following the 2010 census. The Republicans already had control of the Pennsylvania Senate.

Gillespie and Jankowski shared a great insight about control of the US House of Representatives that the Democrats lost sight of in the euphoria of the Obama victory—the party that controls the state legislature controls the drawing of the congressional district boundary lines. They then quietly launched the Republican Districting Majority Plan, known for short as REDMAP, a plan to take control of enough state legislatures to give the Republicans the power to redistrict for the 2012 elections so that they would take control of the US House.

They succeeded. The 2012 elections gave the Republicans 247 seats in the US House of Representatives to 187 for the Democrats. With that margin, the House Republicans were able to block every Obama legislative proposal for the last six years of his administration.

As David Daley reports in his book, *Ratf**ked*, in Pennsylvania, Jankowski focused on two Democratic incumbents as targets for defeat—David Levdansky of Allegheny County and David Kessler of Berks County. In the last two weeks before the election of 2010 every voter in both Levdansky and Kessler's districts received mail accusing the incumbents of selling out their districts by voting to spend $635 million (in a capital budget bill) to build the Arlen Specter Library in Philadelphia.[1]

Neither Levdansky nor Kessler realized what was happening to them until it was too late. Both lost, and the Pennsylvania House of Representatives switched from Democratic control to Republican for the 2010–2012 session.[2]

When the Pennsylvania legislature convened in 2011 the Republicans were in firm control of both the house (112–89) and senate (30–20), as well as the governorship in newly elected Tom Corbett.

The stage was set for a redrawing of the state congressional districts, then seven Democrats and twelve Republicans.

*   *   *

In April of 2011 the US Census Bureau sent the results of the 2010 census for Pennsylvania to the state's Legislative Data Processing Center (LDPC), a nonpartisan service agency of the legislature. After reviewing it, the LDPC forwarded it to the leaders of both parties in both houses. Shortly thereafter, the US House of Representatives certified that Pennsylvania was allocated eighteen seats for the new redistricting, one less than before.

With these prerequisites in hand, the senate Republican leadership assembled a team to draft the legislation needed to establish a new congressional districting plan. Led by Erik Arneson, a key staff assistant to Senator Dominic Pileggi, the majority leader, the group included John Memmi, a veteran Republican staffer knowledgeable in the computer technology of redistricting, two outside consultants, as well as the Philadelphia law firm of Blank Rome, and its redistricting-savvy lawyers. With the use of the autoBound computer software redistricting program,[3] the group behind closed doors drafted a plan as directed by Majority Leader Pileggi and Senator Joseph Scarnati to get as many seats for the Republicans as constitutionally possible.

Scarnati and Pileggi received many contacts from the incumbent Republican congressmen, as well as two Democrats from heavily Democratic districts in Philadelphia and Pittsburgh.

"Absolutely not!" Senator Jay Costa, the Democratic leader, responded when asked if he and the senate Democrats were involved in the drafting of the new maps. "I knew nothing of the new plan until it was offered as an amendment to Senate Bill 1249."

Made public on December 12, 2011, as an amendment to Senate Bill 1249 in the State Government Committee, the bill had only three sponsors, the Republican leadership—Pileggi, Scarnati, and Charles T. McIlhinney Jr., chair of the State Government Committee.

With no public hearings or other opportunity for input from the senate Democrats or anyone else, Senate Bill 1249 moved through the legislature with breathtaking speed. Reported out of the State Government Committee on December 14, it was immediately referred to the Appropriations Committee for a Fiscal Note, and then sent back to the floor, where it was approved on final passage, twenty-six to twenty-four.[4]

There is a saying in the Pennsylvania legislature that if you have the votes you don't need a speech, but if you need a speech you don't have the votes.

That proved true in both the senate and the house, where Democrats made a number of speeches and offered amendments, all in vain. No Republican spoke on behalf of the bill.

In the house, the bill was referred to the State Government Committee on the same day, December 14, and reported to the floor the next day, December 15. Five days later, December 20, the bill received final passage in the house by an overwhelming vote of 136 to 61. The Republican governor signed the bill into law on December 22, 2011, as Act 131.

Few bills in the history of the Pennsylvania legislature have been approved as quickly as Senate Bill 1249.

*   *   *

Soon after Senate Bill 1249 became law, the LDPC added the new congressional plan to the website "Pennsylvania Redistricting," www. redistricting.state.pa.us. The website, maintained by the LDPC, shows the maps and a statutory text of every congressional redistricting back to 1942. This is valuable information for those looking ahead to the next redistricting. Unfortunately, the LDPC did not post anything about the plan in Senate Bill 1249 because of the short time span in which Senate Bill 1249 was acted upon.[5]

*   *   *

With the enactment of Senate Bill 1249, REDMAP achieved a notable success in Pennsylvania. In the next election, 2012, the number of Republicans in the Keystone State's congressional delegation went from eleven to thirteen, and the Democrats went from seven to five.

To understand why, study the map of Pennsylvania's congressional districts in Figure 1.1 or as shown on the Pennsylvania Redistricting website. This is the map drawn by Senate Bill 1249.

A closer look at three of the districts is helpful in understanding what was done.

Start with the seventh congressional district in southeastern Pennsylvania, where four counties that have traditionally been solidly Republican, are now trending toward the Democrats.

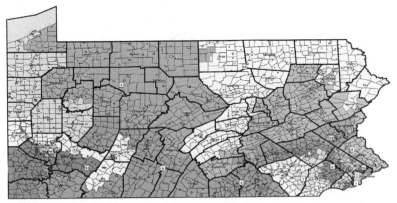

Figure 1.1. Pennsylvania Congressional Districts following the 2010 census (photo: Commonwealth of Pennsylvania).

Delaware County, a former bastion for the GOP, had elected Democrats Bob Edgar and then Joe Sestak to the US House of Representatives. The new version of the seventh congressional district appears to be drawn to preclude another Democrat being elected from Delaware County.

The new seventh district still has most of Delaware County, but it also has a bizarre piece of Montgomery County, sections of central and southern Chester County (although they are not contiguous), a bit of eastern Lancaster County, and an ink-spill blotch of Berks County. See the map of the seventh district in Figure 1.2.

Can the seventh district map be explained other than as a bold effort to make this a safe Republican seat? In 2016 the voter registrations for this district were 226,002 Republicans, 164,163 Democrats, and 63,657 others. The incumbent Congressman Patrick Meehan in 2016 won with 59.47 percent of the vote.

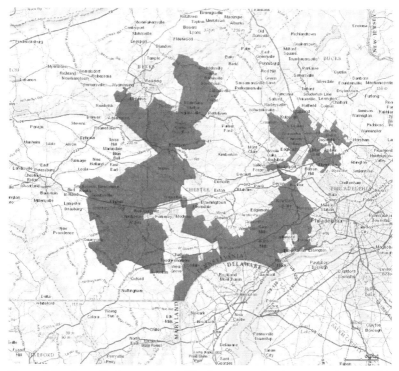

Figure 1.2. Seventh Congressional District, Pennsylvania, 2011 (photo: Wikimedia Commons).

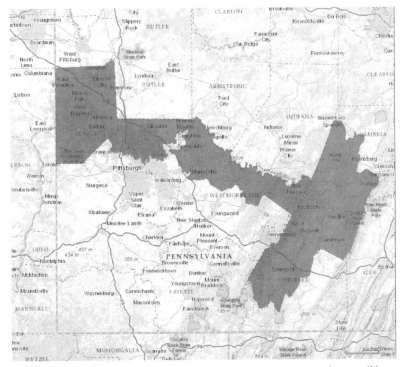

Figure 1.3. Twelfth Congressional District, Pennsylvania, 2011 (photo: Wikimedia Commons).

In western Pennsylvania, the twelfth congressional district drawn in 2012 shows similar characteristics of partisan manipulation of the map.

Originally based in Cambria County, home to the late Congressman John Murtha, the 2011 redistricting manipulated the lines so that Murtha's successor, Mark Critz, had to face off against another incumbent Democrat Congressman, Jason Altmire, and then confront Keith Rothfus, the Republican candidate. Rothfus won. The map in Figure 1.3 shows why.

The district starts on the Ohio border with Beaver and a slim sliver of Lawrence County, takes in northern Allegheny and Westmoreland Counties, before swinging north to include southeastern Cambria and south to northwestern Somerset County. This deftly revised district eliminated two Democratic congressmen and replaced them with a Republican.

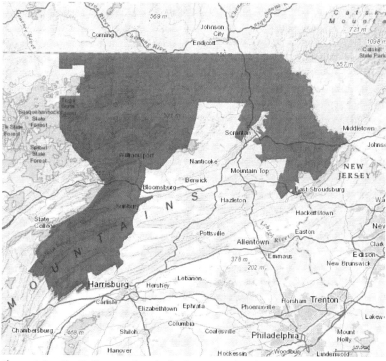

Figure 1.4. Tenth Congressional District, Pennsylvania, 2011 (photo: Wikimedia Commons).

The registration numbers in this district are 198,631 Republicans, 218,707 Democrats, and 59,431 others. These figures might appear to give the Democrats an edge, but they are misleading. The voting patterns of the district are such that in drawing the 2011 maps, the Republicans figured this to be a safe Republican seat. In the 2016 election, the Republicans won with 61.76 percent of the vote.

The tenth congressional district starts southwest of Lewistown, Mifflin County, in the center of the state, extends northwest through four counties to the New York border, and then east to the Delaware River and then south along the New Jersey boundary to Stroudsburg, Monroe County. A crow flying directly from Lewistown to Stroudsburg would travel half way across the state and cross over two other congressional districts.

The registration here is 208,451 Republicans, 128,333 Democrats, and 53,709 others. In the 2016 election, the incumbent Republican, Thomas Marino, received 70.17 percent of the vote.

Turning back to the state as a whole, there are currently 8,450,669 registered voters in Pennsylvania—4,051,103 Democrats and 3,235,781 Republicans and the balance spread among third parties. In the 2016 election, the eighteen Republican candidates received 54 percent of the votes and won 72 percent of the congressional seats, thirteen of eighteen. The Democratic candidates combined collected 46 percent of the vote to win 28 percent of the seats.[6]

Twelve of the eighteen winning candidates received 60 percent or more. Three—two Republicans and one Democrat—had no opponent. The lowest percentage vote was 53.78 for Republican Lloyd Smucker in an open seat in the sixteenth district.

The *Cook Political Report*, a respected national publication, reports that for the 2018 elections, eleven of Pennsylvania's Congress seats are noncompetitive. Of the seven others, only one (the seventeenth) is rated as *leaning Democratic*. Four are scored as *leaning Republican*—the sixth, seventh, eighth, and fifteenth. The fifteenth, now held by Congressman Charlie Dent, will be vacant because of his announced retirement. Two others—the sixteenth and the eighteenth are considered *likely Republican*, even though the eighteenth is vacant because of Representative Timothy Murphy's departure.[7]

Compare these winning margins with those of the winning statewide candidates. Trump won with 48.5 percent, Republican US Senator Pat Toomey with 48.75 percent, Democrat Joshua Shapiro became attorney general with 51.39 percent, Democrat Eugene DePasquale for auditor general with 50.01 percent, and Democratic Joe Torsella became state treasurer with 50.06 percent.

Shapiro, the statewide candidate with the highest winning percentage of 51.39, was 2.34 percent below the lowest percentage for a congressional candidate.

By measuring the vote share received by each party's congressional candidates against the seats won, Pennsylvania has an efficiency gap (explained in chapter 4) of 16.2 percent in favor of the Republicans.[8]

"Is the congressional redistricting plan of Senate Bill 1249 gerrymandering?" I asked Drew Crompton, chief of staff to the senate president and general counsel to the majority caucus. "That depends," Crompton responded. "If using the power of our majority in a constitutional manner to increase the number of our party's seats, it could be. It is political hardball. But it is all constitutional. Until courts tell us otherwise there is nothing wrong with what we did. We have nothing to hide."

Friendly and not at all defensive about how he sees the Republican use of the redistricting process, Crompton continued. "We are here to elect Republicans, not Democrats. That's reality. But the Democrats had their say. We were contacted by [Bob] Brady (Philadelphia Democratic chairman and congressman) and [Michael] Doyle (Pittsburgh congregant). In fact, we needed [Tina] Tartaglione's (Democratic senator from Philadelphia) vote to get the bill out of committee. But you are right, on final passage every Democrat voted against it."

PENNSYLVANIA AS A BENCHMARK FOR OTHER STATES

This anatomy of the last congressional redistricting that was done in Pennsylvania provides a number of measuring points for your state or any of the other forty-three states where redistricting is an issue.

- Is the redistricting plan developed in secrecy?
- What is the level of transparency from the development of the plan through its approval?
- Are there public hearings on the proposed plan before it is voted on?
- Does the minority party have a meaningful role in developing the plan?
- How many of the congressional seats in the plan are competitive? Noncompetitive?
- What is the efficiency gap for your state's congressional delegation?
- Does your state make available easily accessible information on redistricting, such as the Pennsylvania Redistricting website?
- Do you agree with Drew Crompton?

Is Pennsylvania's congressional districting plan gerrymandered? What do you think?

Special Note: January 18, 2018, the Pennsylvania Supreme Court ruled 5–2 that the state's Congressional districting plan enacted in 2011 (described above) violated the "free and equal elections" clause of the state constitution. The Court ordered the legislature and Governor to present a satisfactory new plan by February 15 or it would draw a new map itself.

The legislature and Governor failed to produce a map that satisfied the Court and it drew a new map to take effect for the elections of 2018 and 2020. The legislative Republicans appealed to the US Supreme Court, which denied the appeal. The state Supreme Court order is now final.

Brought by the Pennsylvania League of Women Voters as lead plaintiffs, this case is probably a landmark decision in gerrymandering law in the United States. For the first time, those seeking a new Congressional districting plan went to the state courts and relied solely on state law. The traditional way to challenge a gerrymandered plan was to go to the federal courts under the 14th amendment or the federal Voting Rights Act.

It was an audacious decision, but the Pennsylvania Supreme Court wrote its own declaration of independence from the federal law and courts in gerrymandering cases. Whether it can be done in other states depends in large measure on the constitution of each state.

NOTES

1. Arlen Specter was a five-term Republican US Senator, considered too liberal by many Republicans. His support from Republicans was so low that in 2010 he ran for reelection in the Democratic primary but lost to Joe Sestak. He died October 14, 2012. The library is now the Arlen Specter Center for Public Service at Thomas Jefferson University in Philadelphia.

2. There were nine other Democrats defeated as well.

3. There are two popular software programs used by redistricting drafters—autoBound and Maptitude. They are readily available through their website listings.

4. The Republicans had thirty votes, the Democrats twenty. Four Republicans voted against the bill, presumably because the way the bill carved up their counties. Every Democrat voted no.

5. This is a contrast to the LDPC's reporting on the work of the Legislative Reapportionment Commission that does redistricting for the state house and senate. Throughout the meetings of the commission, the LDPC posted reports of its meetings and proposed plans. Commission meetings are public.

6. Michael Wereschagin, "The House Always Wins," *The Caucus*, January 24, 2017, 7.

7. "2018 House Race Ratings," *The Cook Political Report*, July 7, 2017.

8. David A. Lieb, "Redrawing America," *Associated Press*, July 22, 2017.

Chapter Two

Elbridge Gerry's Bum Rap and How We Got to Where We Are

Redistricting of state legislative and congressional boundary lines on an unequal basis within a state is as old as our republic. Since the colonial era, redistricting was not based on population, but rather on representation of municipal units, usually counties or towns. This was a natural carryover from the British practices in forming legislative seats.

As Supreme Court Justice Felix Frankfurter wrote, in Great Britain at the time the US Constitution was written, the sole basis for representation in the House of Commons was local geographical units, such as boroughs.[1] Each county or borough elected a fixed number of representatives to Parliament regardless of population.[2]

The American colonies, and later the states, used the county or town as the basic measure of representation in legislative seats. With the county as the measuring unit, it was simple to use redistricting to the advantage of the district designers.

Governor Patrick Henry of Virginia did not want his political adversary James Madison elected to the first US House of Representatives under the new constitution in 1788. Henry made sure that Orange County, heavily populated with anti-federalists, was added to the district, thus making it unlikely Madison would be elected. In spite of Henry's machination, Madison ran an astute campaign and won by 336 votes out of 2,280 cast.[3]

In 1790 the lower portion of South Carolina, with a voting population of less than 29,000, elected twenty senators and seventy house mem-

Figure 2.1. Elkanah Tisdale, "The Gerry-Mander," *Boston Gazette*, March 26, 1812

bers, while the rest of the state, with a voting population of more than 111,000, elected only seventeen senators and fifty-four representatives.[4]

In Maryland, the county system of legislative allotment produced a legislature in 1820 in which 200,000 people were represented by eighteen members while 50,000 had twenty.[5]

While this kind of disproportionate representation had become the usual politics of the new nation, Massachusetts Governor Elbridge Gerry inadvertently had his name attached to it when he signed into law the new state senate redistricting plan in 1812. The plan, as shown in the cartoon in Figure 2.1, began in Chelsea in the southwest and extends

Figure 2.1.   Elkanah Tisdale, "The Gerry-Mander," *Boston Gazette*, March 26, 1812 (retouched). Frequently reproduced, "this new species of monster" has forever linked partisan redistricting to Elbridge Gerry. Tisdale's cartoon was reproduced in the *Salem Gazette*, April 2, 1813, with the following text. It raises issues that have never been resolved.

Again behold and shudder at the exhibition of this terrific Dragon, brought forth to swallow and devour your liberties and equal Rights. Unholy party spirit and inordinate love of power gave it birth;—your patriotism and hatred of tyranny must by one vigorous struggle strangle it in its infancy. The iniquitous Law, which cut up and severed this Commonwealth into Districts, is kindred to the arbitrary deeds of Napoleon when he partitioned the territories of innocent nations to suit his sovereign will. This Law inflicted a grievous wound on the Constitution,—it in fact subverts and changes our form of Government, which ceases to be Republican as long as an Aristocratic House of Lords under the form of a Senate tyrannizes over the People, and silences and stifles the voice of the Majority.

When Tyranny and arbitrary Power thus make inroads upon the Rights of the People, what becomes the duty of the citizen? Shall he submit quietly and ignominiously to the decrees of the Usurpers? Are the citizens of this Republic less jealous of their rights than their ancestors? Will you, then, permit a Party to disfranchise [*sic*] the People,—to convert the Senate Chamber into a Fortress in which ambitious office-seekers may entrench themselves and set at defiance the frowns of the People? No,—this usurping Faction must be dislodged from its strong-hold.

Arise, then, *injured Citizens!* Turn out! Turn out! Let Monday next be the day of your Emancipation—by one manful Struggle reclaim your usurped Rights—and frown into obscurity those audacious men who unblushingly boasted—"We have secured the Senate for ten years, and should have been fools if we had not done it." Prove on election day that the Folly of their men is equal to their want of honesty and contempt of the People. Elect patriots who will be loyal to the Constitution, and faithful to the interests of the State.

---

around Boston through nine other towns to Salisbury in the northeast. A cartoonist saw the figure as a salamander but changed it to "Gerrymander." Gerry's party won 50,164 votes to take twenty-nine seats, while the opposition received 51,766 votes but only eleven seats.[6]

Is the Massachusetts senate redistricting of 1812 worse than that of South Carolina in 1790? Maryland in 1820? Virginia in 1788?

It does not really matter. Because of a well-targeted cartoon Governor Gerry's place in US history is irrevocably tarred with the redistricting practices of the era. Overlooked and largely unappreciated is Gerry's career as an authentic American patriot. He signed the Declaration of

Figure 2.2. John Trumbull, *Declaration of Independence*, 1819, is a monumental (12 × 18 ft.) oil painting in the US Capitol rotunda. It shows the moment on June 28, 1776, when the first draft of the declaration was presented to the Second Continental Congress meeting in Philadelphia in what is now known as Independence Hall. Trumbull made most of the portraits from life. Elbridge Gerry is the fourth in the group of ten seated figures at the far right of the painting. Later Gerry would refuse to sign the Constitution. He believed it gave the executive branch too much power (photo: Wikimedia Commons).

Independence,[7] attended the Constitutional Convention of 1787, served as governor of his state, and was vice president while James Madison was president.

That the United States should move into the nineteenth century with such a widespread pattern of inequity in legislative and congressional representation is really no surprise. The US Constitution that provides for the Congress is silent on how the states shall allocate the US House seats within each state.

One of the great divisive issues the Constitutional Convention confronted in 1787 was how the colonies would be represented in the new national legislature—equally by state or by population? The largest colony, Virginia, had a total population of 747,610. Delaware, the smallest in population, had about 59,094.[8]

After extended debate, the delegates compromised. Each state, regardless of population, would have two US Senators to be chosen by the state legislature,[9] and each state would be allocated seats in the House of Representatives based on population.

The implementing language of the compromise is in Article 1, Sections 2 and 4, of the Constitution.[10] The number of seats for each state is to be determined every ten years. The times, places, and manner of holding elections for the US House "shall be prescribed in each State by the legislature thereof."

That is it, all the Constitution as ratified in 1788 said on the drawing of congressional boundary lines. Whatever the delegates to the Constitutional Convention said in their deliberations was not brought into the document. In effect, the state legislatures were left to carry on as before in drawing congressional district boundary lines.

For the next 174 years—seventeen census/redistricting cycles—states' legislative drawing of their own seats, as well as congressional seats, went unchallenged. Seen as a political thicket, courts viewed redistricting with trepidation. In the federal judicial system, courts were powerless to intervene even if they wanted to. Federal courts had no jurisdiction to hear a case on redistricting. The Constitutional silence in Article 1 precluded seeking relief in a federal court.

On July 9, 1868, the states ratified the Fourteenth Amendment to the US Constitution. A major policy of the Republican-controlled Congress, and most states, the amendment contains five sections designed to assure that the newly freed slaves would not lose their federal rights at the hands of southern state governments following Reconstruction.

Section 1 provides:

> All persons born or naturalized in the United States, and subject to the jurisdiction thereof, are citizens of the United States and of the State wherein they reside. No State shall make or enforce any law which shall abridge the privileges or immunities of citizens of the United States; nor shall any State deprive any person of life, liberty, or property, without due process of law; *nor deny to any person within its jurisdiction the equal protection of the laws.*[11] (Emphasis added by the author.)

At the time of its ratification no one saw the new amendment as having anything to do with legislative or congressional redistricting.[12] In fact, it took ninety-two years for aggressive lawyers to seize upon the Equal Protection Clause (emphasized in the text) as a basis for giving federal courts the jurisdiction to hear redistricting cases.

The case started in Tennessee, where the state legislature had apportioned legislative seats by its ninety-five counties, regardless of population, pursuant to a 1901 statute. Nashville had grown significantly, but its representation at the state capitol remained unchanged. The mayor of Nashville, and other voters, asked a federal district court to declare the 1901 statute unconstitutional because it deprived them of equal protection of the law as provided in the Fourteenth Amendment.

There were twenty-three times more voters in a Nashville legislative district for every voter in the rural counties. In other words, the voting power of one in a rural county was the same as twenty-three in the city.

The district court dismissed the case for lack of jurisdiction, and the plaintiffs appealed to the Supreme Court.

The Supreme Court reversed the district court, holding that the complainants had stated a valid claim under the Fourteenth Amendment and were entitled to a trial and decision.

Over the fierce opposition of Felix Frankfurter, the court held that federal courts had jurisdiction to hear redistricting cases when there was a claim of denial of equal protection under the Fourteenth Amendment.

With this holding, *Baker v. Carr*,[13] the Supreme Court began the ending of the two-century-old practice of state legislatures to redistrict without regard to population. Like the court's decision in *Brown v. Board of Education*[14] that overruled *Plessy v. Ferguson*[15] to end racial segregation in schools, *Baker v. Carr* changed forever the almost casual way in which legislatures, free of legal challenge in federal court, drew their district boundary lines.[16]

The federal courts now had jurisdiction to hear cases on state legislatures' handling of redistricting.

The significance of this was not lost on Felix Frankfurter, the court's most passionate opponent of granting jurisdiction to hear redistricting cases. In the first conference of the justices to review the case after it was argued by the parties, Frankfurter addressed his colleagues for ninety minutes, inveighing against getting the federal court into the political thicket of state legislatures and their politics. When the court made its decision, Frankfurter wrote the sixty-page dissenting opinion, discussed earlier.

Figure 2.3. Felix Frankfurter, associate justice of the Supreme Court, 1939–1962, was a staunch advocate of judicial restraint. He feared the court would get entangled in politics if it were to adjudicate the states' apportionment of state legislative and congressional districts (photo: 1939, Washington, DC; Harris & Ewing Photographic Services, Collection of the Supreme Court of the United States).

Baker v. Carr gave federal courts jurisdiction to hear redistricting cases, but it did not provide a standard by which federal courts could measure claims of constitutional impairment by redistricting. That came in a new case a year later from Georgia, *Gray v. Sanders.*[17]

Sanders, a qualified voter in Fulton County, asked a federal district court to invalidate Georgia's county-unit system of tabulating votes in Democratic primary elections for statewide offices. According to its population, each county was allocated votes on a sliding scale that tilted in favor of the smaller counties. The vote of an individual citizen decreased in meaning as the county population increased. When Sanders brought his suit, a combination of votes from the counties with the smallest population gave counties with only a third of the total state population a clear majority of county unit votes.

The Supreme Court, relying on the Equal Protection Clause of the Fourteenth Amendment, declared that once a geographical unit has been chosen from which governmental representation is to be elected, all voters in that district must have an equal vote.

Speaking through Justice William O. Douglas, the court laid down a rule for measuring compliance with the Fourteenth Amendment's Equal Protection Clause that forever transformed how redistricting maps would be drawn.

> When a state exercises power wholly within the domain of state interest, it is insulated from federal judicial review. But such insulation is not carried over when state power is used as an instrument for circumventing a federally protected right.
>
> The conception of political equality from the Declaration of Independence, to Lincoln's Gettysburg Address, to the Fifteenth,[18] Seventeenth,[19] and Nineteenth[20] Amendments could mean only one thing—*one person, one vote.*[21] (Emphasis added by author.)

Like a great bolt of lightning, this decision struck the redistricting practices of the states with great force and leveled them. It destroyed the traditional, almost routine systems of redistricting based on counties, towns, and other governmental units. State legislatures had to start anew to redistrict.[22]

There was more to come from the US Supreme Court. A year later the court rules invalid a Georgia congressional plan based on a 1931 statute in which the congressman from one district represent two to three times more people than other districts. Justice Hugo Black, after holding that reapportionment is not a political question, added:

> The right to vote is too important . . . to be stripped of judicial protection.
> . . . The 1931 Georgia apportionment grossly discriminates against voters in the Fifth Congressional District. . . . it has contracted the value of some votes and expanded the value of others . . . If the Federal Constitution intends that when qualified voters elect members of Congress each vote be given the same weight as any other, then this statute cannot. We hold . . . as nearly as is practical one man's vote in Congressional elections is to be worth as much as any others.[23]

The one person, one vote rule, however, gave a great advantage to the map drawers. It is simple. Voters are tangible units that can be counted and allocated with relative ease. The only limitation was that each district had to have the same population—no deviation among the districts.

With that limitation, the mapmakers could draw the districts in any shape they wanted. The map drawers were in a new world of redistricting. There was, however, one more complication for the map drawers. February 8, 1870, the states ratified the Fifteenth Amendment, the voting rights amendment.

> Section 1. The right of citizens of the United States to vote shall not be denied or abridged by the United States or by any State on account of race, color, or previous condition of servitude.
>
> Section 2. The Congress shall have the power to enforce this article by appropriate legislation.

Nine decades later it became obvious to the Congress that this article was ignored and disregarded in some states. The brutal treatment by the Alabama police of the civil rights marchers in Selma and the murder of three civil rights workers in Mississippi who had sought to increase black voter registration cried out for corrective action.

Under the strong leadership of President Johnson, the Congress enacted the Voting Rights Act of 1965.[24] This act did not create new voting rights for blacks and other minorities. That had already been clearly provided for in the Fifteenth Amendment. The act sought, as provided in Section 2 of the amendment, to give the federal government tools to enforce those rights.

Figure 2.4. President Lyndon Johnson celebrates with Rosa Parks, Martin Luther King, Jr., Ralph Abernathy, and other civil rights leaders after signing the 1965 Voting Rights Act into law. The law was immediately hailed as a "triumph for freedom." It authorizes the Department of Justice to remedy violations of the Fifteenth Amendment of the Constitution, which prohibits the denial of the right to vote "on account of race, color, or condition of previous servitude" (photo: August 6, 1965, Washington, DC; CORBIS/Corbis via Getty Images).

After repeating the voting rights of the Fifteenth Amendment, Section 2, the act, in Section 5, gave special enforcement powers to the Department of Justice in those areas where voter discrimination appeared to be the greatest.

Section 5. Prohibited some states from implementing changes affecting voting until the changes were approved by the Attorney General or local US District Courts.

With this act, the cause of racial justice for the second time had a great impact on state legislative redistricting.[25] When the Congress held hearings on bills to extend the act for five and then seven years, there was extensive testimony on how some states manipulated legislative and congressional boundary lines to prevent newly registered black voters from effectively using their ballots.[26]

The map drawers in several states, such as North Carolina and Texas, which struggled to deal with these new requirements, produced numerous redistricting plans that were litigated.[27]

In 2013, the Supreme Court brought voting rights enforcement under the act to a virtual halt. In *Shelby County v. Holder*, the court ruled unconstitutional the formula on which the *preclearance* requirements were based.[28]

The Voting Rights Act is in limbo, but the *Shelby County v. Holder* decision did not reduce the voting rights of blacks or any other minority. It did block the federal enforcement of these rights with the tools of the act. Redistricting plans can still be challenged as violating the Fifteenth Amendment, although this places the burden of proof on the complainant.

The one person, one vote ruling of the Supreme Court and the Voting Rights Act are the last federal government directives to state legislatures on redistricting. But two other developments have had an equally strong impact on redistricting—computer software programs and the dark money made possible by the Supreme Court decision, *Citizens United v. Federal Election Commission.*

Computer software programs have revolutionized the drawing of congressional and legislative boundary lines. What previously took months to do can now be done in a few days.

As Drew Crompton, chief of staff to the Pennsylvania Senate president and general counsel to the majority caucus, told me, "In the nineties, redistricting maps took months, in 2001 it took a few weeks, and for the 2011 maps it took only a few hours. For the 2021 maps? It could be a matter of minutes. It is really stunning!"

What makes the computer software programs so incredibly helpful to the map drawers is the data used in the programs. In earlier days, the only information available to map drawers was the US census data, voter registration lists, and figures for each voting district. The legislative leadership in each state and the redistricting staff did it themselves.

But now the data collected and made available by computer programming companies goes far beyond that—census figures, population trends, voting patterns by party, income levels, employment and unemployment, population trends, ethnic and racial patterns, age groups, and frequency of voting.[29]

This data is easily processed and applied to the map as directed by the map makers. The programs are so sophisticated that they can draw maps that conform to the boundaries of census blocks, the smallest geographic unit used by the US Census Bureau.

The legislative leadership and staff need outside help to handle this, and now software consultants, redistricting-savvy consultants, and redistricting knowledgeable lawyers are essential to preparing the new maps.

With this kind of staffing support, the software is an effective tool for those with the political power to put their maps into legislative form and make it the law of the state.

How effective is the tool? So good that only one congressional seat has changed hands since the 2011 maps were drawn in the states of Ohio, Pennsylvania, Michigan, North Carolina, and Wisconsin.[30] (These are among the states targeted by the Republican State Leadership Committee in REDMAP, discussed in chapter 1.)

Computer software programs and databases are available to anyone who wants to buy them, not just the map drawers for the major parties.[31] There are also a number of groups that offer draw-it-yourself redistricting maps free of charge. (Information on them is provided in the Citizen's Toolbox on page 71.) A word of caution, however.

Using redistricting software programs, whether purchased or free of change, at the level needed to transfer the resulting map into a statute is not simple. Only a handful of people in each state have the knowledge and sophistication to do the work adeptly. A novice in redistricting using the industry accepted standard software programs would be like a new pilot licensed to fly single-engine airplanes taking the controls of a two-engine jet.

Nevertheless, use of the do-it-yourself redistricting programs is a good step forward to understanding what is involved.

* * *

The US Supreme Court has made one other decision that dramatically impacts redistricting, but not directly. On January 21, 2010, the court gave birth to dark money in US politics by ruling that the federal election law's restrictions on the amount and preelection timing of independent expenditures by corporations and unions violated the free-speech provision of the First Amendment.[32] The court invalidated those restrictions.

Citizens United is a nonprofit corporation organized and funded by the Koch brothers and their network to promote their goals of reduced taxes and less governmental regulation. In early 2008 Citizens United released a documentary called *Hillary: The Movie*, which was an independent expenditure. Its intended use could have violated the restrictions in the federal election law and subjected Citizens United to significant financial penalties. Citizens United sought to prevent the Federal Election Commission (FEC) from enforcing this law. It asked a district court to enjoin the FEC from applying the law to *Hillary: The Movie* and to declare the independent expenditure prohibition unconstitutional.

The district court denied Citizens United request, but the Supreme Court reversed the ruling and launched unlimited independent expenditures from anonymous donors.

The Supreme Court ruled that independent expenditures by corporations do not give rise to corruption or give the appearance of corruption. Moreover, the court declared there is not sufficient governmental interest justifying limits of the political free speech of nonprofit corporations.

Citizens United won its case, *Hillary: The Movie* was widely distributed, and funds from undisclosed donors to nonprofits started to flow.

As David Daley reported,

> big donors were no longer limited to capped donations to the party or a candidate. They could go big, and now Gillespie and Jankowski had the perfect plan. The Republicans would mount a comeback (from Obama's election in 2008) from the states.[33]

The impact of the *Citizens United v. FEC* case on congressional redistricting is discussed at greater depth in chapter 3.

*   *   *

Where are the fifty states of the United States on congressional redistricting today? It depends on which state you are in.

In seven states—Alaska, Delaware, Montana, North Dakota, South Dakota, Vermont, and Wyoming—redistricting is not an issue. Those elect only one member each to the US House of Representatives.

Thirty-seven states' legislatures have retained control of drawing the redistricting maps.[34] But in six states—Arizona, California, Hawaii,

Idaho, Montana, New Jersey, and Washington—the redistricting is in the hands of an independent commission.

California has the independent commission most removed from the legislature and the two major parties. It is the polar opposite of Pennsylvania, a classic example of assertive partisanship in congressional redistricting.

The California Citizens Redistricting Commission (CRC) was created by the public approval of Proportion 11 in the 2008. Similar proposals had been rejected four times, but in 2008 it obtained 51 percent of the vote, thanks to the leadership of a coalition of citizens' organizations led by Common Cause and the campaigning of Governor Arnold Schwarzenegger.

Proposition 20 approved in the 2010 elections added congressional redistricting to the work of the CRC. The CRC succeeded in defeating two legal challenges to its validity and went to work.

For its first redistricting map drawing, the CRC blazed new ground in public participation in the process. More than 2,700 citizens participated in thirty-four public meetings in thirty-two locations, and 20,000 citizens submitted comments.[35]

The districts drawn by the CRC as a result of this process are in place. A new CRC will be constituted for the cycle beginning with the 2020 census, and a similar process will be used.

Completely separated from the legislature, California's redistricting method is the total opposite of Pennsylvania's. To appreciate how far the California CRC is removed from its legislature, consider how the CRC is appointed.

The CRC has fourteen members—five Democrats, five Republicans, and four declined-to-state—in a unique manner. Thirty thousand persons wanting to serve on the CRC submitted an online application. Those considered qualified are invited to submit a supplemental application in which they answer questions in essay form. Auditors from the state's audit bureau select 120 from these applications—forty Democrats, forty Republicans, and forty declined-to-state. Following interviews, the 120 are reduced to sixty, and the names are given to the leaders of both parties in both houses of the legislature. The legislative leaders, like trial lawyers picking a jury, have peremptory rights to remove twenty-four from the pool. The audit bureau then randomly draws three Democrats, three Republicans, and two declined-to-state from the pool. The eight selected

Figure 2.5. California Citizens Redistricting Commission Committee Meeting, 2017. Some members participated by telephone (photo: October 27, 2017, Sacramento, CA; author).

pick six more from the pool, two from each party and declined-to-state. These fourteen serve for a ten-year term, and their work is supported in line-drawing years by a staff of fourteen full-time employees. The CRC is funded by a legislative appropriation, and in nonline-drawing years has a budget of $93,000 for the fiscal year 2017–2018.[36]

The CRC maintains an informative website, www.wedrawthelines. ca.gov. Click on "See the Video" for a twenty-minute discussion of the CRC and how it works.

Each state must be analyzed on its own and that is beyond the scope of this book. But it is relatively easy to do with any state.

The National Conference of State Legislatures (NCSL) maintains a comprehensive website on redistricting, both state and congressional. In the Citizen's Toolbox, "Redistricting Criteria for Each State"[37] is a state-by-state description of the criteria used for both state and congressional redistricting, together with citations to the state constitutional and statutory provisions. This is Document D in the Citizen's Toolbox.

The NCSL also has a list of the initiative and referenda states that shows the process and requirements for the states. See Document E in the Citizen's Toolbox.

The NCSL website also has "Redistricting Commission: Congressional Plans"[38] that provides a summary of the law in the six states with independent commissions and three states with advisory commissions. (See Document F in the Citizen's Toolbox.) Another section shows all legislation currently pending in state legislatures on independent commissions: "Redistricting Commission Bills."[39]

The NCSL documents just described are reprinted in the Citizen's Toolbox, except the one on redistricting bills.

There is also redistricting information on each state's website. To access this, use your browser or search engine to enter the state's name followed by "redistricting."

You can then browse your state's election bureau (often found in the secretary of state's office for the state) for the official election results for congressional races and maps of the congressional districts. See if your state has a separate website, as Pennsylvania does, that is devoted exclusively to redistricting and provides history and maps on the congressional districts.

There are many other sources of information available about each state. The Citizen's Toolbox contains a list of some of those sources in Document B.

With this information, you can begin to evaluate how well your state does with congressional redistricting. How does it compare to Pennsylvania? To California? Are there changes in your state's congressional redistricting system you would like to make? If there are, the next two chapters tells you what is involved and the challenges you will confront.

NOTES

1. Dissenting opinion in Baker v. Carr, 369 U.S. 186 (1962) at 266. Frankfurter's opinion is a well-documented summary of redistricting in US history, and the author has freely relied on it in this chapter.

2. This was immortalized in parody by lyrics in Sir John Porter's song in Gilbert and Sullivan's operetta *H. M. S. Pinafore*, "I grew so rich that I was sent by a pocket borough into Parliament. I always voted at my party's call and never thought of thinking for myself at all."

3. "Madison's Election to the First Federal Congress," *Founders Online*, July 20, 2017. Madison's opponent was James Monroe. This was the only time in US history when two future presidents ran against each other for Congress.

4. *Baker*, 369 U.S. at 310 (Frankfurter, J., dissenting).

5. Ibid.

6. David Daley, *Ratf**ked: The True Story behind the Secret Plan to Steal America's Democracy* (New York: Liveright, 2016), xviii.

7. In Trumbull's great mural of the signing of the Declaration of Independence, Gerry is number twenty on the list of signers at the bottom.

8. "1790 United States Census," *Wikipedia*, September 2, 1790.

9. With the ratification of the Seventeenth Amendment in 1913, US Senators are to be chosen by popular election.

10. The texts of these provisions is found in the Citizen's Toolbox that follows chapter 5.

11. The full text of the section of the Fourteenth Amendment is found in the Citizen's Toolbox in Document A.

12. *Baker*, 369 U.S. at 310 (Frankfurter, J., dissenting).

13. *Baker*, 369 U.S. 186 (1962).

14. Brown v. Board of Education, 347 U.S. 483 (1954).

15. Plessy v. Ferguson, 163 U.S. 537 (1896).

16. "More Perfect—The Political Thicket," audio transcript, Radio Lab. Available at http://www.radiolab.org/story/the_political_thicket. This is the most fascinating document the author uncovered in researching for this book. It has the voices of Earl Warren, Felix Frankfurter, and William Douglas.

17. Gray v. Sanders, 372 U.S. 368 (1963).

18. Right to vote, ratified February 3, 1870.

19. Election of senators by popular vote rather than by the state legislature. Ratified April 8, 1913.

20. Women's right to vote. Ratified August 18, 1920.

21. *Gray*, 372 U.S. at 381.

22. At least twenty states guaranteed each county at least one seat in one of the legislated houses regardless of population. *Baker*, 369 U.S. at 319 (Frankfurter, J., dissenting). Pennsylvania was one of them. When I was elected to the Pennsylvania House of Representatives in 1966, about one quarter of my district was Montour County, a whole county that previously elected its own representative.

23. Westberry v. Sanders, 376 U.S. 1(1964).

24. See "Voting Rights Act of 1965—Overview," *FindLaw.com.*

25. The first was the enactment of the Fourteenth Amendment, with its Equal Protection Clause. As noted earlier, it took almost a century before this provision had its impact on redistricting.

26. "Voting Rights Act of 1965—Overview," *FindLaw.com.*

27. For examples, see Robert Barnes, "After Losses on Voting Laws and Districting, Texas Turns to Supreme Court," *Washington Post*, August 27, 2017.

28. Shelby County v. Holden, 570 U.S. 2 (2015).

29. This is information available from public records.

30. David Daley, "How Will Big Data Change Gerrymandering?" *Salon*, April 15, 2017.

31. A popular redistricting program is offered by Caliper. Its Maptitude for Redistricting, including one state of data, is priced at $10,000 per licensee. This is the industry-preferred software for legislative redistricting. They also offer a standard Maptitude for $695 and a redistricting database (one state) for $2,500. For additional information, go to www.caliper.com.

32. Citizens United v. Federal Election Commission, 588 U.S. 310 (2010).

33. Daley, *Ratf**ked*, 12.

34. Iowa has a unique redistricting system. Its redistricting plans are developed by a nonpartisan staff that submits the plans without political or election data, including the addresses of incumbents. Since the legislature must approve the plans, it is included in the thirty-seven states with legislative control.

35. Common Cause Brief in Radanovch v. Bower, no. S196852. Copy supplied to author by Common Cause.

36. Correspondence from Christina Shupe, senior operations manager of the CRC.

37. http://www.ncsl.org/research/redistricting/redistricting-criteria.aspx

38. http://www.ncsl.org/research/redistricting/redistricting-commissions-congre...

39. http://www.ncsl.org/research/redistricting/redistricting-commission -bills.aspxicin

Chapter Three

Reform through the Legislature— An Uphill Struggle and Dark Money

How to obtain reform of the congressional redistricting process through the legislature depends on which state you are in. In twenty-four states the legislature has exclusive jurisdiction over redistricting. But the other twenty-six states have a form of citizen initiative and referendum process that allows citizens to seek change without the legislature.[1]

STATES WITHOUT AN INITIATIVE AND REFERENDUM PROVISION

Pennsylvania, like Illinois and Texas,[2] is a major state in which bills have been introduced to change congressional redistricting. The thrust of the Pennsylvania bills is to take congressional redistricting off the hands of the legislature and give it to an independent commission.[3]

When I sat down with Carol Kuniholm, Fair Districts PA's president, she had just finished her speech to a regional meeting of the National Association for the Advancement of Colored People (NAACP) in the Sheraton Harrisburg. The mother of two grown daughters and a former youth pastor, Kuniholm has a keen sense of direction and confidence that the campaign will succeed.

Her work for Fair Districts PA she told me "is more than a full-time job!" The only time she takes off is Saturday evenings and Sunday.

Her involvement began in December 2015 while serving as the League of Women Voters of Pennsylvania director on election reform.

She regularly participated in weekly telephone meetings with other groups to talk about what they could do. Redistricting and gerrymandering became the center of their conversation, but the group had no sense of organization or urgency. Some wanted to study it for six months, and others wanted to engage a computer programmer to set up a website.

Frustrated by the lack of urgency and focus, Kuniholm took charge of the efforts by putting together a website within a month and choosing the name Fair Districts PA after she had some contact with Fair Districts Florida and Ohio. The coalition behind it included the League of Women Voters, Common Cause, and the Committee of Seventy in Philadelphia.

At the time she launched Fair Districts PA, a bill to create an independent commission for redistricting had already been introduced by State Senator Lisa Boscola, a Democrat from Northampton County. (Later State Representative David Parker, a Republican from Monroe County, introduced a companion bill in the house of representatives.)

Enactment of these bills became the goal of the coalition. Kuniholm organized meetings, conducted dozens of conference calls, and kept updating the website. Momentum built, but the legislative session ended without passage of the bills.

In 2017, she continued undeterred. The speech to the NAACP was her twenty-sixth of the year. As Fair Districts PA was being launched, she had a fear of public speaking, did not think she could do it. Fully determined, she overcame her doubts and plunged into the speaking circuit, delivering the Fair Districts PA message all over the state.

At the time of our lunch, Fair Districts PA had held 200 meetings in 2017 and had an email membership of 11,000. It has no paid staff; all of the work is done by volunteers.

As for the passage of Senate Bill 22 or House Bill 722 in the current legislative session, she is confident one of them will pass. "We have until June 2018." (Deadline for advertising the proposed constitutional amendments for its first session passage.)

Meanwhile, Fair Districts PA continues to hold public informational meetings such as the one I attended in Hershey in October. The feature of the program was Jeff Reichert's seventy-minute motion picture, *Gerrymandering*, an informative, entertaining documentary that ranges from Governor Arnold Schwarzenegger campaigning for Proposition 11 in California in 2009 to the fifty-three Texas House Democrats who took up residence in the Holiday Inn in Ardmore, Oklahoma, in 2003 to avoid a quorum to gerrymander the Texas congressional delegations.

After the screening, Fair Districts PA volunteers distributed pre-printed postcards and literature and urged the crowd to contact their state legislators. They offered to pay the postage for the postcards.

Other help is on the way according to Kuniholm. David Thornburgh, president and CEO of Committee of Seventy in Philadelphia, is developing a "Draw the Map" computer program. Students and the public will be invited to draw districting maps in statewide competitions.

Thornburgh was one of the featured speakers at a statewide conference on gerrymandering that Kuniholm organized and chaired in Harrisburg on October 14, 2017. Over 270 attended and heard speeches from Kathay Feng of the California Common Cause and Thomas Wolf from the Brennan Center for Justice, as well as Thornburgh.

Kuniholm believes firmly that public awareness is essential to achieving the reform she seeks and will press on. She is indefatigable.

* * *

In my earlier conversation with Drew Crompton, I asked about Kuniholm and the Fair Districts PA campaign.

"Fair Districts PA is doing what they should be doing at the grassroots level—they are working hard," he responded. "The problem I have with their proposal [Senate Bill 22] is that it would give control of congressional redistricting to a group of novices—who may have no understanding of the state politics or government."

"Just because they have a 'D' or 'R' after their name doesn't mean they will know what they are doing," Crompton added. "I could understand adding some citizens to a commission that included legislators. That would make more sense than what they [Fair Districts PA] are seeking."

Crompton offered no indication that Senate Bill 22 would be considered.

Robert Jubelirer, a Republican senator from 1975 through 2006, and a veteran of three redistrictings, told me he sees no chance for an independent commission to be approved in Pennsylvania. "It will never happen. The political opposition is too great."

This is not surprising. According to the NCSL, in 2017 there are twenty-three states where bills have been introduced for independent commissions:[4] Delaware, Florida, Georgia, Illinois, Indiana, Kansas, Kentucky, Maryland, Massachusetts, Michigan, Minnesota, Nebraska,

New Hampshire, New Mexico, North Carolina, Ohio, Oregon, Pennsylvania, South Carolina, Tennessee, Texas, Utah, and West Virginia. None of this legislation has been enacted.

STATES WITH AN INITIATIVE AND REFERENDUM PROCESS

In the twenty-six states that have an initiative and referendum procedure, it is considerably easier, but not free from difficulty, to obtain reform of the congressional redistricting method. The NCSL has produced a list of such states that includes a description of the type of referendums in each such state. This is found in Document E of the Citizen's Toolbox. You will see that what is available through the initiative and referendum process varies from state to state.

Florida does not have an initiative or referendum on legislation, but it does permit citizens to go directly to the ballot box with state constitutional amendments.

In the 2010 election, Florida voters approved an amendment to their constitution that reads:

> [In congressional redistricting] no apportionment plan or individual district shall be drawn with the intent to favor or disfavor a political party or an incumbent; and districts shall not be drawn with the intent or result of denying or abridging the equal opportunity of racial or language minorities to participate in the political process or to diminish their ability to elect representatives of their choice; and districts shall consist of contiguous territory.[5]

Note that this language does not remove the congressional redistricting power from the state legislature, but it does mandate standards for the exercise of that power. In other words, the state added its own standards to those of the federal constitution of one person, one vote from the Fourteenth Amendment and the prohibition of racial discrimination in voting under the Fifteenth Amendment.

Getting that language approved and then implemented proved to be a strenuous ordeal for its proponents. Pamela Goodman, a successful businesswoman and president of the League of Women Voters of Florida, was involved from the beginning. She remembers it well.

"There were two constitutional amendments on the Florida ballot in 2010," she told me, "Amendment 5 for the state legislature and Amendment 6 for congressional."

"The amendments were drafted by two outstanding constitutional lawyers in Florida, but had to be summarized in twenty-seven words to go on the ballot."

To place a constitutional amendment on the ballot requires a petition signed by 1 percent of the vote in the last election. In this case, Goodman continued, "we had to get 750,000 verified signatures. Our Florida secretary of state reviewed the petition to ascertain that the signatories were registered to vote and not duplicates."

"But we first had to obtain 75,000 signatures and submit it to the state supreme court for review and certification. After that, we had two years to gather the other 675,000 signatures. To do this, 30 percent of the petition circulators were volunteers and the other 70 percent were professionals our coalition employed."[6]

How much did this cost you? I inquired. "My estimate is it cost $3–4 million to get the amendments on the ballot and then another $3–4 million for the litigation to get it implemented after it was approved by the voters. Our advocacy funds were raised by the coalition. Ellen Freidin led the effort."[7]

"There was huge, aggressive opposition from the legislature. It did everything it could think of to defeat the amendments."

"One tactic they used was to get its own amendment on the ballot to confuse voters, but it failed to meet the requirements."

Goodman believes the opposition spent $10 million to defeat the amendments.

The voters approved the proposed amendments with 63 percent (3.1 million), three percent more than the 60 percent minimum needed for constitutional amendments.

Still, Goodman continued, "the Republican legislative majority persisted in its efforts to thwart the amendment after the voters approved it. First, Governor Scott sought to stop implementation and then litigation ensued."

As Davis Daley reported:

After approval of the amendment the Republican legislative leadership undertook an audacious, secret, complicated scheme to thwart it. This plot was uncovered and made public by the litigation to which Goodman refers.[8]

"We were in court thirteen times before the opposition had to stop," Goodman added.

In 2015 the Florida State Supreme Court approved the congressional maps the citizens' coalition had drawn because the legislature was unable to do it. That map is now the congressional plan for Florida.[9]

"The court ruled for our map because it found that the state legislature could not do it themselves."

Another lawsuit on the amendment came from Congressman Mario Diaz-Balart and Congresswoman Corrine Brown, a Republican and a Democrat.

They argued that the under Article 1, Section 4 of the US Constitution the district line had to be drawn by the legislature. The court denied their relief.[10]

"Brown had the most gerrymandered seat in the state," Goodman observed, "and that was the juggernaut of litigation."

"Our legal fees to defend the implementation of Amendment 6 in all of the cases were high—several million," she noted.

Was all of the toil, stress, and effort to enact Amendments 5 and 6 worth it? I asked.

"Absolutely! 200 percent. I would do it all over again in a flash."

Why?

"The level of discourse by our legislators and congressmen it has raised. They have districts where they have to pay attention to a broader spread of voters. We started an evolution, not a revolution. We do not see radical changes in our redistricting, but we are now moving in the right direction."

Goodman went on. "I do not favor an independent commission to draw the lines. Such commissions are only as good as the appointing officials, most likely just as partisan as now. What we did in Florida has reset the rules for redistricting, but still leaves the actual line drawing to the legislature. We can challenge any map they draw if it violates the new constitutional rules."

What is your advice to citizens in other states?

"It can be done! It requires public awareness, hard work, and unyielding persistence. But the power is with the voters, and they can do it . . . a persistent effort, but it can be done."

"Gerrymandering and redistricting at first seem geeky and complicated," she explained, "but they are really simple once understood."

Florida did not use its initiative and referendum process to obtain an independent commission for redistricting, but Arizona did. The state legislature was so opposed that it fought to invalidate the amendment all the way to the US Supreme Court.

During the 2000 election, the voters of Arizona approved Proposition 106 by a 53.1 percent to 46.9 percent margin, 784,272 to 612,676 votes.

Proposition 106 amended the state constitution to take out of the legislature's hands the redistricting power and transferred it to a five-person Arizona Independent Redistricting Commission (AIRC) of two Democrats, two Republicans, and an independent.

Applicants for the commission are appointed by the appellate court board. From the lists of qualified applicants, the legislative party leaders select the Democratic and Republican members, who in turn choose the chair from the list of independents.

For the 2010 census cycle the four partisan members of the AIRC chose Colleen Coyle Mathis of Tucson as the independent chair. Mathis volunteered for the job as public service, but found that it ran her through an ordeal of enormous pressure, hours of raucous public hearings, name calling, impeachment by the Republican state senate (summarily reversed within hours by the state supreme court), and an investigation by the state attorney general.[11]

Mathis is not a quitter, and she did not quit. She served through the current redistricting and continues as the chair of the AIRC. The most important event during Mathis's tenure is undoubtedly the decision of the US Supreme Court in *Arizona State Legislature v. Arizona Independent Regulatory Commission.*[12]

Like the Florida legislature's opposition to its Proposition 6, the Arizona legislature based its case on the argument that only the state legislature has the redistricting power under Article 1, Section 4 of the US Constitution. By creating the AIRC, the legislature argued, the voters violated the Constitution's Elections Clause, "The Times, Places and Manner of holding Elections for Senators and Representatives, shall be prescribed in each State by the Legislature thereof."

This fundamental question placed at stake all independent congressional redistricting commissions. If the Arizona legislature prevailed, other independent congressional redistricting commissions would be invalidated. Not surprising, the California Citizens Redistricting Commission filed a friend of the court brief in support of the AIRC.

The court ruled five to four in favor of the AIRC and thereby saved other independent commissions and those that might be created in the future. Justice Ruth Bader Ginsburg wrote for the majority.

The people of Arizona turned to the initiative to curb the practice of gerrymandering and, thereby, to ensure that Members of Congress would have "an habitual recollection of their dependence on the people." The Federalist No. 57, at 350 (J. Madison). In so acting, Arizona voters sought to restore "the core principle of republican government," namely, "that the voters should choose their representatives, not the other way around." Berman, Managing Gerrymandering, 83 Texas L. Rev. 781 (2005). The Elections Clause does not hinder that endeavor.

In Arizona, Florida, and California, the right of voters to change congressional redistricting through the initiative and referendum was, after a long battle, upheld. But that does not guarantee that similar efforts in other states will do as well.

South Dakota voters in 2016 approved a referendum to create an independent ethics commission, limited lobbyists' gifts to legislators, prohibited public officials from joining lobbying firms for two years after leaving office, and created "Democracy vouchers" for voters to steer toward their favored candidates.

Three months later, the legislature passed, and the governor signed, a bill to repeal the referendum. The legislature accomplished this by using an "emergency" clause in the state constitution. In signing the repeal bill, Governor Dennis Daugaard, claimed "the public had been hoodwinker by scam artists who vigorously misrepresented the proposed measures."[13]

The experiences in California, Florida, Arizona, and South Dakota make an important point: congressional redistricting reform is easier in states with an initiative and referendum process, but it is not easy. Wendy Underhill, the redistricting expert at the NCSL, summarized it well. "It's a long way from having an idea to getting it in front of the voters by collecting signatures . . . it will take hard work and considerable funding." Each state has its own laws for initiatives and referendums. To proceed you need to research and understand what your state requires.

Figure 3.1.   Ruth Bader Ginsburg, associate justice of the Supreme Court, 1993–. Her opinion in *Arizona State Legislature v. Arizona Independent Redistricting Commission* upheld the constitutionality of independent redistricting commissions (photo: January 5, 2016, Washington, DC; Steven Petteway, Collection of the Supreme Court of the United States).

Looking forward, there are now four states where ballot referendums on congressional redistricting are now pending and may be on the 2018 ballot—Michigan, Ohio, South Dakota, and Utah. Ohio's proposed referendum is well underway to the 2018 general election ballot. Certified by the attorney general, an energetic drive led by Fair Districts Ohio has begun to collect the necessary 305,591 signatures of registered voters in at least forty-four of the state's eighty-eight counties.[14]

The proposed amendment to the Ohio constitution would transfer the power to draw congressional district lines from the state legislature to the bipartisan Ohio Redistricting Commission approved by the voters in 2015 to draw the lines for state legislative districts. Under the proposed amendment, the commission will draw the congressional district lines to conform with standards for minimizing partisan advantage, geographical compactness, and avoiding the splitting of municipal subdivisions. The overall plan must have some correlation with the statewide vote of each party. Finally, a redistricting plan requires the approval of two minority party members of the commission.[15]

This referendum portends to make Ohio the battleground of a sharp clash in the 2018 election on the issue of legislative control of congressional redistricting. Here is why.

Ohio's congressional delegation is currently twelve Republicans and four Democrats. This is the result of the operation REDMAP described earlier in chapter 1. The current congressional map of Ohio was drawn in secrecy by the Ohio Republican legislative leadership and the Republican National Committee.[16] There was no participation by the Democratic Party or public input.

The proposed amendment is in total conflict with the manner in which the current congressional lines in Ohio were drawn. This is a clear threat to the Republican iron grip on the US House of Representatives and also an opportunity for the Democrats to get a level playing field in Ohio congressional races.

The Republican National Committee and the Koch network, who strongly want ultraconservatives to keep control of the US House of Representatives, can be expected to seek the defeat of the amendment. On the other side, the national Democrats will be spending funds to get the proposal approved. They were caught sleeping in 2010 by the Republicans and their operation REDMAP. They will not repeat that mistake.[17]

Carrie Davis, executive director of the League of Women Voters of Ohio and one of the leaders of the Fair Districts Ohio campaign, is energetic and well-focused on their goal. She told me they fully expect a strong effort to defeat the proposal in 2018. Like Kuniholm in Pennsylvania, Davis is confident of success.

"This is not our first rodeo!" she exclaimed to me. "We have been through this before. We will be ready."

Davis recalled the 2005 election in which a ballot measure, similar to the one that will be on the 2018 ballot, was defeated through a strong effort of the US House Speaker, John Boehner, also a congressman from Ohio. "He collected and spent $7.5 million to defeat the proposal."

The stakes in Ohio are high, and this will likely be a bitterly fought campaign. But there is one development that might change it. September 22, 2017, the Ohio Republican legislative leadership announced the creation of a working group to study the congressional redistricting issue and make recommendations. One can only speculate as to what the working group and legislature will do. Fair Districts Ohio and its volunteers are reaching out to state legislators and asking them to work together. But Davis said she and Fair Districts Ohio will continue their campaign to get their proposal on the general election ballot.

Ohio will be the center of attention from all around the country until the outcome is decided.

*   *   *

The advocates of change in their state's congressional redistricting system—whether by an act of the legislature or through a ballot initiative—can expect to be opposed by the immense, but virtually invisible, power of dark money.

The reason is simple. If Fair Districts PA (seeking a legislative action) or the Ohio Fair Districts (proposing a ballot referendum) succeed in their efforts to take the congressional map drawing from their state legislature, that would be a real threat to the present Republican control of the US House of Representatives.

Pennsylvania now has thirteen Republican congressmen and five Democrats, while the Ohio delegation is twelve Republicans to four Democrats. The proposed changes in those states could easily put in play twelve safe Republican seats.

This is all related to the redistricting that will take place in 2022, following the 2020 census. This will be the first complete national redistricting since 2012, when the Republicans took control of the House that is still in effect.

There are huge stakes in this for Charles and David Koch and their network of wealthy, ultraconservative partners in their political venture. For several decades before 2010, the Koch brothers and allies like Richard Mellon Scaife spent considerable time and money advocating their beliefs in smaller government, lower taxes, and reduced regulations, especially environmental regulations. Their efforts were largely confined to founding and funding nonprofit organizations like Americans for Prosperity and the Heritage Foundation. Contributions directly to candidates and campaign committees were limited in amount by the federal election law and required disclosure of the donor's identities. Corporations were prohibited from spending for political purpose.

This changed radically with the *Citizens United v. FEC* decision of the US Supreme Court in 2010. As discussed earlier (see chapter 2), now corporations can spend unlimited amounts in independent expenditures, spending uncoordinated with a candidate or campaign committee. This unloosed a flood gate for anonymous spending by nonprofit corporations organized under Sec. 501(c)(4) of the Internal Revenue Code. Such contributions are tax exempt, and the donor's identity may be undisclosed. Persons of great wealth, like the Kochs, established their own foundations, made tax-exempt contributions to them, and then had them make independent expenditures in political campaigns.

While not the only ones taking advantage of this opportunity, the Kochs and their allies have become the masters of dark money. They used it astutely and to good effect. In fact, they developed their own private political party, quite separate from the Republican Party.

In 2016 the Kochs' private network of political groups had a bigger payroll than the Republican National Committee. The Koch network had 1,600 paid staffers in thirty-five states and boasted that its efforts covered 80 percent of the population. This marks a huge escalation from just a few years earlier. As recently as 2012, the Kochs' primary political advocacy group, Americans for Prosperity, had a paid staff of only 450.[18]

How much will the Koch network spend to stop congressional redistricting reform? It is impossible to say before it happens. But the money is there.

In 2015 Charles Koch estimated that his groups had a budget of $750 million for two years, of which $250 million would go for politics.[19]

Figure 3.2A. David Koch, Koch Industries executive vice president and Americans for Prosperity Foundation chairman, gives a thumbs-up to Republican presidential candidate and former Godfather's Pizza CEO Herman Cain during the Defending the American Dream Summit at the Washington Convention Center (photo: November 4, 2011, Washington, DC; Chip Somodevilla/Getty Images).

Figure 3.2B. Charles Koch, head of Koch Industries, during an interview about his book *The Science of Success* (photo: February 26, 2007, Wichita, KS; Bo Rader/Wichita Eagle/MCT via Getty Images). The Koch Brothers have used their vast wealth to advance their political views through educational programs as well as independent expenditures.

* * *

The Koch network will not be alone in contesting—or supporting—changes to the congressional redistricting systems of the states between now and 2022. They will, of course, spend time and money to elect state legislators who support their cause.

Others with the same interest as the Kochs include Karl Rove, with his Crossroads American Foundation, and the US Chamber of Commerce. The Republican National Committee is certainly going to have an updated version of REDMAP in play.

Democrats at the national level will also enter the fray. They will not repeat their mistake of 2010 in ignoring state legislative races.

The Democratic National Redistricting Committee as of July 30, 2017, had raised $10.8 million.[20]

David Cohen, a veteran of the Obama campaigns, in early September, launched Forward Majority. The goal is to give to state legislative races the same kind of support now given to Democratic candidates for federal office under the Senate and House Majority PACs.

Forward Majority began its efforts by investing $1 million in state house elections in Virginia held in November 2017. Cohen also expects to invest $100 million in two states in the next four years.[21]

* * *

Available past independent expenditure reports give some idea of what to expect going forward.

In the 2013–14 period, a record of $372 million from all spenders, not just the Kochs, was spent in twenty-nine of the fifty state elections.[22] (The other twenty-one states lacked the reporting requirements to provide information on those states.)

Independent expenditures in state elections by the Koch network or anyone else is not reported to the FEC, which deals only with federal elections. Independent expenditures need to be reported only to the state where they are spent, and only to the extent required by the state.

That is the rub, if you want to find out who is making independent expenditures in your state, how much they are spending, and for what purpose they are spending it.

"It's a mess" trying to follow the money in state elections, Denise Roth Barber, managing director of the National Institute on Money in State Politics, told me.

"Even with a staff of twenty-three," she explained, "following the money at the state level is difficult. The Federal (spending) is easy. The problem is that not all states have reporting requirements and in those that do there is great inconsistency."

As a result, the National Institute on Money in State Politics reports on selected states. Even there it is not possible to separate legislative spending from others. For example, a report may show spending on mailings, but not specify the candidates it was spent for or against.

The National Institute on Money in State Politics has produced a scorecard map that gives a grade to each of the fifty states on whether they have essential disclosure requirements for independent spending.

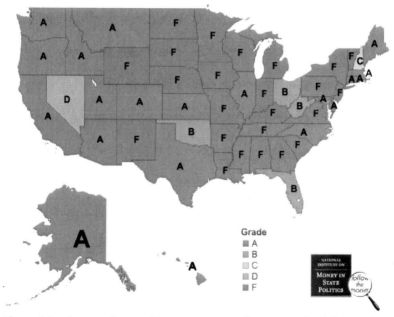

Figure 3.3. Scorecard map, 2014. It scores each state on the fullness of its required reporting of independent expenditures (photo: National Institute on Money in State Politics).

The results are stunning.

Nineteen states are scored A.
Four are B.
One is a C.
One is a D.
Twenty-four are graded F.

The scores are based on several criteria:

Are independent expenditures required to be reported?

The scope of the required reporting.

Must the spender identify the target of the spending?

Does the state require the spender to state its position?

Must the reporting independent spender disclose the intent of its contributors?

(This will not provide the names of donors to nonprofit corporations organized under Sec. 501(c)(4) of the Internal Revenue Code. They are covered by federal law. The states lack the power to require this. The states may, however, require a Sec. 501(c)(4) nonprofit to report otherwise.)

How does your state score? After reviewing the map, go to Document G in the Citizen's Toolbox for the criteria grade for each category used by the National Institute on Money in State Politics to determine the overall grade for each state.

*   *   *

The efforts to reform congressional redistricting in each state face considerable opposition. But, as this chapter suggests, there is more than the opposition to contend with. How are the citizens to know who is spending money to defeat or elect candidates to the state legislature, or to defeat or approve ballot measures? The National Institute on Money in State Politics has made it quite clear—there is a need for reform of independent expenditures reporting requirements in many states. Regardless of how you feel about the congressional redistricting question in your state, you can still ask your state legislators to change the reporting requirements to full disclosure. That is an essential part of a sound election system, and it is a worthy cause for every citizen.

NOTES

1. Alaska, Arizona, Arkansas, California, Colorado, Florida, Idaho, Illinois, Maine, Maryland, Massachusetts, Michigan, Mississippi, Missouri, Montana, Nebraska, Nevada, New Mexico, North Dakota, Ohio, Oklahoma, Oregon, South Dakota, Utah, Washington, and Wyoming.

2. Texas has a particularly stormy history of controversy on meeting the Constitution requirements in redistricting. See, for example, Robert Barnes, "After Losses on Voting Laws and Districting, Texas Turns to Supreme Court," *Washington Post*, August 27, 2017. In 2003 the Texas House Democrats went to the Holiday Inn in Ardmore, Oklahoma, to avoid voting on a new congressional plan sought by Tom DeLay, the Republican congressional leaders from Texas.

3. Senate Bill 22 and House Bill 722 of the 2017–18 session. For the text of the bills, go to the Pennsylvania General Assembly website and insert the bill numbers under "legislation."

4. Go to the NCSL website under "Redistricting Commission Bills" for a list of the states and a description of the bills in each state.

5. Now Article III, Sec. 20(a) of the Florida Constitution.

6. The coalition was the League of Women Voters of Florida and Common Cause Florida.

7. Ellen Freidin, a lawyer in Miami and chair of Fair Districts Florida, was a driving force for the enactment of Amendments 5 and 6.

8. David Daley, *Ratf**ked: The True Story behind the Secret Plan to Steal America's Democracy* (New York: Liveright, 2016), 120–34.

9. Mary Ellen Klas, "Florida Supreme Court Approves Congressional Map Drawn by Challengers," *Miami Herald*, December 2, 2015.

10. Jay Weaver, "Florida Judge Upholds Florida Redistricting Amendment," *Tampa Bay Times*, September 9, 2011.

11. Daley, *Ratf**ked*, chapter 10, that is a detailed report of the AIRC and its creation.

12. Arizona State Legislature v. Arizona Independent Regulatory Commission, 576 U.S. ___(2015).

13. "Report of Gregory Krug," CNN, February 2, 2017.

14. See the Fair Districts Ohio website for more on the campaign.

15. See the Fair Districts Ohio website for the text and summaries of the proposal.

16. Daley, *Ratf**ked*, 83–98.

17. Before leaving office, President Obama set up a National Democratic Redistricting Committee led by Eric Holder, his former attorney general, to reclaim state legislative seats for the Democrats, and thus the power to draw congressional district lines. Please visit their website for more details.

18. Jane Mayer, *Dark Money: The Hidden History of the Billionaires behind the Rise of the Radical Right* (New York: Anchor Books, 2016), xvii.

19. "Interview with Kai Ryssdal," Marketplace radio program, October 2, 2015.

20. Daniel Marans, "Democratic Super PAC Steps Up Push to Fight 'Conservative Dark Money,'" *Huffington Post*, September 28, 2017.

21. Ibid.

22. Calder Burgam, "Independent Spending Overview, 2013 & 2014" (National Institute on Money in State Politics), *FollowtheMoney.org*, November 17, 2016.

Chapter Four

Judicial Relief—A Firm Maybe

That the Supreme Court of the United States will dramatically change the rules for congressional and state legislative district map drawing is now a real possibility. In the case of *Gill v. Whitford*, argued before the court on October 3, 2017, the plaintiffs propose a new standard for measuring the constitutionality of redistricting—the efficiency gap standard (to be explained next).

It is difficult to overstate the importance of this case to redistricting. The case has the potential to reshape US politics, both in the state and national capitols.

In late July Justice Ruth Bader Ginsburg said that the court's decision to hear the case was perhaps the most important (decision) on the gerrymandering issue.

"So far, the court has held race-based gerrymandering as unconstitutional but has not found a manageable, reliable measure of fairness for determining whether a partisan gerrymander violates the Constitution," she said.[1]

The significance of the case is shown by the fact that no less than forty-six *amicus* (friend of the court) briefs were filed,[2] in addition to the briefs of the parties to the case. Those filing friends of the court briefs include the State of Texas, the Republican National Committee, the Legacy Foundation, the League of Woman Voters, the American Jewish Committee, the NAACP Legal Defense and Educational Fund, Senators John McCain and Sheldon Whitehouse, and a Bipartisan Group of 65 Current and Former State Legislators.[3]

Figure 4.1. The Roberts Court, 2017. Pictured (left to right) Ruth Bader Ginsburg, Elena Kagan, Anthony M. Kennedy, Samuel A. Alito Jr., John G. Roberts Jr., Sonia Sotomayor, Clarence Thomas, Neil M. Gorsuch, and Stephen G. Breyer (photo: June 1, 2017, Washington, DC; Franz Jantzen, Collection of the Supreme Court of the United States). In spring 2018 the Roberts Court is expected to render decisions on the Wisconsin and Maryland gerrymandering cases. If the rulings establish a standard for measuring excessive partisanship in legislative and congressional representation, they could end the overt partisanship that has dominated those systems since the beginning of the republic. The Roberts Court is poised to revolutionize the way we elect our lawmakers.

The case is from Wisconsin, one of the key states successfully targeted for legislative takeover by the Republican National Committee's REDMAP initiative in 2010.[4]

As described by Robert Barnes of the *Washington Post*, with a firm control of both legislative houses and a Republican governor, the Republicans took full advantage of their opportunity in Wisconsin.

[Legislative] aides were dispatched to a private law firm to keep their work out of public view. They employed the most precise technology available to dissect new U.S. Census data and convert it into reliably Republican districts. Democrats were kept in the dark, and even GOP incumbents had to sign confidentiality agreements before their newly revamped districts were revealed to them. Only a handful of people saw the entire map until it was unveiled and quickly approved.[5]

The Republican efforts paid off for them in the 2012 elections. With 48.6 percent of the statewide votes, they captured 60 percent of the seats in the assembly, sixty of the ninety-nine seats. Two years later the GOP received 52 percent of the vote and 63 percent of the seats.[6]

The challengers to this legislative map drawing scheme found a measure by which to show how overly partisan it is, the efficiency gap standard developed by Professor Nicholas O. Stephanopoulos and Eric McGhee.[7]

The efficiency gap is a mathematic model for determining how unfairly legislative district boundary lines have been drawn. It does this by computing the number of wasted votes by voters of the losing party in a district that has been cracked, or by those of the winning party in districts that have been packed.

Cracked districts are those where the voters of the stronger party have been spread into several districts to dilute the value of the remaining voters of that party. In a packed district the voters of one party have been concentrated to give the party drawing the district lines a strengthened advantage in other districts.

According to Katelyn Ferral of the Wisconsin *Capital Times*, the efficiency gap is calculated by combining into one number the votes in districts that have been packed and those districts cracked. This number is broken down to show the votes wasted and looks at which party has wasted more, based on how the districts were drawn. The larger the number of wasted votes (the efficiency gap), the greater the unfairness is in the redistricting.[8] The efficiency gap is a bit confusing at first impression, but it uses a metric standard that the plaintiffs demonstrated to the satisfaction of the trial court. See Document H in the Citizen's Toolbox for a hypothetical example that shows how the efficiency gap is calculated.[9]

While not as simple as the one person, one vote rule (i.e., every district must have the same number of voters) that is now the basic standard for legislative redistricting, it is sufficiently clear for the federal judges in Wisconsin.

Applying the efficiency gap formula to the Wisconsin legislature, the plaintiffs say the gap for 2012 was 13.2 percent and 9.6 percent in 2014. They argue that gaps over 7 percent violate the US Constitution.[10]

How does this mathematical formula relate to the Equal Protection Clause of the Fourteenth amendment? That is the challenge for the plaintiffs in the Supreme Court. The formula easily demonstrates unfairness in redistricting map drawing, but that is not enough to win the case. The court can only act on the basis of Constitutional provision. How is a 7 percent or more efficiency gap a Constitutional violation? Why not 5 percent or 10 percent?

Indeed, why should there be any deviation from zero? There is no deviation from zero under the one person, one vote rule. Why should there be one here?

Questions like these are the thorns of the political thicket that Justice Frankfurter warned of forty-five years ago. Today the same fears are expressed by conservative columnist George Will.

> [The plaintiffs] want the Court to plunge the Judiciary into unending litigation involving dueling professors who will cherry-pick concentric metrics to serve as standards. [The Wisconsin case] warns about a social science hodgepodge.[11]

If the court adopts the efficiency gap in some form, it will have a huge impact on the 2021 redistricting of state legislative and congressional districts map drawing.

In the 2012 and 2014 elections, twelve state legislatures exceeded more than 10 percent on the efficiency gap standard: Florida, Indiana, Kansas, Michigan, Missouri, New York, North Carolina, Ohio, Rhode Island, Virginia, Wisconsin, and Wyoming.[12]

The Pennsylvania congressional plan has an efficiency gap level of 16.2 percent. Michigan's is 15 percent, and North Carolina's is 19.7 percent.[13]

No one can predict what the court will do with the efficiency gap standard, but it appears to turn on the vote of Justice Anthony Kennedy. In 2002 the Pennsylvania congressional districting plan was challenged in federal court as gerrymandered and unconstitutional. The case of *Vieth v. Jubelirer* went to the US Supreme Court, which ruled against the challengers on a five to four vote.[14]

For the majority, Justice Antonin Scalia said there was no standard by which a court could determine if a legislative districting plan was drawn on excessive partisan lines.

The fifth vote for the majority came from Justice Kennedy, who wrote a concurring opinion saying that he would not foreclose the possibility of a suitable standard in future cases.

Even assuming that the new justice, Neil Gorsuch, will reflect the same views of the now deceased Justice Scalia, the Wisconsin case could still be upheld and become applicable in all fifty states. The key vote could be Justice Kennedy and whether he sees the efficiency gap as a satisfactory standard.

Robert Jubelirer, then the president of the Pennsylvania Senate, was the lead defendant in *Vieth v. Jubelirer.* I asked how he viewed the case today, especially in light of the Wisconsin case now before the court.

"I remember it well," he told me. "Kennedy used the pornography test for determining the unconstitutionality of a redistricting plan. His words were 'I'll know it when I see it.'"

Jubelirer believes the court will have a hard time with the Wisconsin case. "It is a very difficult issue because it is so very subjective."

No one knows how the court will rule until it does. As explained in the next chapter, however, regardless of what the court does, there will be a great deal of work for reform of the congressional district map drawing in the states. Until the court renders its decision, however, everyone relying on the court is relying on a firm maybe.

* * *

After this chapter was written, the Supreme Court on December 8, 2017, agreed to take a second case on gerrymandering in its current

Figure 4.2. Anthony M. Kennedy, senior associate justice of the Supreme Court, 1988–, is likely to be the swing vote in the upcoming decision on gerrymandering in states' redistricting (photo: June 19, 2001, Washington, DC; Eileen Colton, Collection of the Supreme Court of the United States).

judicial term. The justices decided to hear a case from Maryland, *Benisek v. Lamone*, in which Republicans challenge the constitutionality of the Democratic-controlled legislature's redistricting of the state's sixth congressional district. In the Wisconsin case, the challengers are Democrats against a Republican-controlled legislature. The case differs from the Wisconsin case in two other ways. First, the challenge is based on an alleged violation of the First Amendment's freedom from retaliation doctrine and not an Equal Protection Clause violation claim as in Wisconsin. The other difference is that the Maryland case challenges only one congressional district, not the entire state redistricting plan.[15] The Wisconsin and Maryland cases may be combined and decided in decisions announced simultaneously.

NOTES

1. Aaron Liptak, "On Justice Ginsburg's Summer Docket: Blunt Talk on Big Cases," *New York Times*, August 1, 2017, A13.
2. Briefs filed by persons not actually parties to the case, but who have interest in the outcome.
3. For the complete list of these briefs, and to read any of them, go to the Supreme Court's blog site, http://www.scotusblog.com/case-files/cases/gill-v-whitford. The author is one of the friends of the court in the brief filed by the Bipartisan Group of 65 Current and Former State Legislators.
4. See David Daley, *Ratf**ked: The True Story behind the Secret Plan to Steal America's Democracy* (New York: Liveright, 2016), chapter 9, for a graphic description of how this was done.
5. Robert Barnes, "Wisconsin Redistricting Effort Could Shape Future U.S. Elections," *Washington Post*, June 11, 2017, online edition.
6. Liptak, "On Justice Ginsburg's Summer Docket," A3.
7. Nicholas O. Stephanopoulos and Eric M. McGhee, "Partisan Gerrymandering and the Efficiency Gap," *The University of Chicago Law Review* 82 (2015): 831–900.
8. Katelyn Ferral, "Understanding Wisconsin's Legislative Redistricting Trial: The Efficiency Gap, Partisan Symmetry, and More." *The Capital Times*, May 28, 2016.
9. This example calculation was prepared by the Brennan Center for Justice at New York University and is titled "How the Efficiency Gap Works." It is the best explanation the author found.
10. Liptak, "On Justice Ginsburg's Summer Docket," A3.

11. George Will, "Will the Supreme Court Fall Into a Political Thicket?," *Washington Post*, October 1, 2017.

12. Adam Liptak, "Justices to Hear Major Challenge to Partisan Gerrymandering," *New York Times*, June 19, 2017, citing a 2015 report by Simon Jackman, a redistricting expert.

13. David A. Lieb, "Redrawing America," *Associated Press*, July 22, 2017.

14. Vieth v. Jubelirer, 541 U.S. 267 (2004).

15. Robert Barnes, "Supreme Court Will Take Up a Second Gerrymandering Case This Term," *The Washington Post*, December 9, 2017.

Chapter Five

The Necessity for Citizens to Act

Our voice as a body politic is no longer represented in the halls of Congress. Neither the US Senate nor the US House of Representatives can be said to reflect the opinion of our citizenry.

From the beginning the Senate was to represent states, not population. The great compromise of the 1787 Constitutional Convention gave each state two senators regardless of its population. When the Constitution was adopted the population of the thirteen states totaled 3,929,212. Virginia had the largest population—747,610—and Delaware had the smallest, 59,094.[1] Virginia had twelve times the population of Delaware, and the Constitution writers gave each two senators.

Today the population of the fifty United States is 323.1 million. The largest state is California with a population of 39.25 million, and the smallest is Wyoming with a population of 585,000.[2] Each has two senators and the population ratio between the two is sixty-five to one. (In the *Baker v. Carr* case discussed earlier the ratio in state legislative seats was twenty-three to one.) The population representation distortion in the US Senate is such that about half of the US population gets 80 percent of the seats and the other half 20 percent.[3]

To change the two senate seats per state provision of the US Constitution is not feasible, certainly not in the foreseeable future. To do that requires Congress by a vote of two thirds in each house to propose the amendments and then have it ratified by three fourths of the state legislatures. Or two thirds of the state legislature could apply to Congress to call a new Constitutional convention.[4] Neither of these ways to amend the US Constitution is presently a serious possibility.

We need, therefore, to look to the US House of Representatives that, unlike the Senate, was intended to represent the population. But as this book, and the writings of many other authors has shown, the US House no longer represents the American public. In the 2016 elections the Republicans won 55.2 percent of the seats with slightly less than 50 percent of the vote.[5] As noted earlier in this book, since the 2012 elections the ultraconservative caucus of the GOP has such a lock on the majority leadership in the US House that it blocked every legislative initiative of President Obama for the last six years of his tenure. The ice-cold grip of the ultraconservative caucus forced the resignation of the House Speaker, John Boehner, when he sought to work out a compromise with President Obama. The ultraconservative lock is still such that it blocks almost every effort by the majority Republicans or the Trump Administration to pass substantive legislation.

We cannot change the Senate, but we can do something about the House to make it such that it genuinely represents our opinion. We can do that only by focusing on our state legislatures, where the power to draw congressional district lines resides.

As pointed out in chapter 4, what can be done to reform congressional redistricting by the states will be greatly affected by what the Supreme Court does in the Wisconsin gerrymandering case.

If the court rejects the plaintiffs and their proposed efficiency gap standard, there is no choice for reformers but to carry on the struggle state-by-state as described in chapter 3. The struggle may be more difficult because the legislatures and those who want to keep the present system will feel emboldened in their resolve by the Supreme Court's refusal to intervene.

If, however, the court rules for the plaintiffs and adopts the efficiency gap standard as a new national standard, the work of those seeking reform in congressional district map drawing will be made considerably easier, but still not easy.

The court's opinion will most likely apply only to Wisconsin. It will not be automatically applied to all the states. But the court's decision will be a clear signal to those states with efficiency gaps of 7 percent or more that they need to move to compliance or face litigation to do so.

Getting compliance with the new standard will be a state-by-state challenge. There will be stiff resistance. The defenders of the present systems will do what they can to resolve ambiguities in their favor. To assure compliance the reform-minded citizens in each state must be prepared to press their legislators and to hire lawyers.

Citizens will need to let their legislature know that they expect full and complete compliance with the new standard. They should not hesitate to engage legal counsel for guidance and to prepare to seek a court order for compliance.

The road to success, with or without a favorable Supreme Court decision, will be uphill, time-consuming, and financially expensive. It will be a marathon, not a sprint. There is no simple or easy way to do it.

The information provided in the Citizen's Toolbox that follows this chapter will help you prepare for your effort.

The first step is to evaluate your state's congressional map drawing system and the state's performance in requiring reporting and disclosure of independent expenditures. The Citizen's Toolbox contains the congressional redistricting requirements for each state, the list of initiative and referendum states, the list of states with redistricting commissions, and the evaluation of each state's independent expenditure reporting requirements. Also included is the Brennan Center model for calculating the efficiency gap in your state.

The toolbox also provides online sources of information from foundations and associations that make available to the public their research and reports on redistricting, gerrymandering, and dark money.

The toolbox is helpful, but do not stop with it. Go to websites for your state constitution and state legislature for what they tell about redistricting in your state. Next check the website of the election bureau for your state, usually in the state's department of state, for election returns and campaign finance reports, including independent expenditure reports.

This information enables you to pass judgment on your state's congressional redistricting system. It makes you knowledgeable enough to get into the fray to change it.

If you want to seek a change in your state, join an existing organization seeking the same goals as you. Or take action on your own by meeting with your state representative and senator.

Tell your legislators that you want a reform in the congressional redistricting, as well as, a full reporting requirement for independent expenditures under your state's election law.

Tell your US representative and senators that you want the Internal Revenue Code amended to require the disclosure of the identities of those who contribute to nonprofit corporations that make independent expenditures in political campaigns.

Our future as a nation is dependent on a House of Representatives that truly reflects public opinion and the public interest in dealing with and resolving the many problems before us. The collective impact of the manner in which congressional districts are now drawn has produced a national legislature incapable of doing that.

We cannot and should not tolerate a US House of Representatives that fails to reflect the voice of the American people. We must expunge from our body politic the infection of unlimited anonymous political spending.

Accomplishing this is up to us, the citizens of America. The political power of our country rests with us, and now we need to exert that power.

NOTES

1. "1790 United States Census," *Wikipedia*, September 2, 1790.
2. U.S. Census Bureau, July 20, 2016.
3. Michelle Goldberg, "Tyranny of the Minority," *New York Times*, September 25, 2017.
4. Article V of the US Constitution.
5. Goldberg, "Tyranny of the Minority," citing a Brookings Institution report.

THE CITIZEN'S TOOLBOX

Citizen's Toolbox Contents

Document A

US Constitutional Provisions

ARTICLE 1—LEGISLATIVE

Section 1

All legislative Powers herein granted shall be vested in a Congress of the United States, which shall consist of a Senate and House of Representatives.

Section 2

The House of Representatives shall be composed of Members chosen every second Year by the People of the several States, and the Electors in each State shall have the Qualifications requisite for Electors of the most numerous Branch of the State Legislature.

No Person shall be a Representative who shall not have attained to the Age of twenty-five Years, and been seven Years a Citizen of the United States, and who shall not, when elected, be an Inhabitant of that State in which he shall be chosen.

Representatives and direct Taxes shall be apportioned among the several States which may be included within this Union, according to their respective Numbers, which shall be determined by adding to the whole Number of free Persons, including those bound to Service for a Term of Years, and excluding Indians not taxed, three fifths of all other Persons. The actual Enumeration shall be made within three Years after the first Meeting of the Congress of the United States, and within every subsequent Term of ten Years, in such Manner as they shall by Law direct. The Number of Representative shall not exceed one for every thirty Thousand, but each State shall have at Least one Representative; and until such enumeration shall be made, the State of New Hampshire shall be entitled to chuse three, Massachusetts eight, Rhode-Island and Providence Plantations one, Connecticut five, New-York six, New Jersey four, Pennsylvania eight, Delaware one, Maryland six, Virginia ten, North Carolina five, South Carolina five, and Georgia three.

When vacancies happen in the Representation from any State, the Executive Authority thereof shall issue Writs of Election to fill such Vacancies.

* * *

Section 4

The Times, Places and Manner of holding Elections for Senators and Representatives, shall be prescribed in each State by the Legislature thereof; but the Congress may at any time by Law make or alter such Regulations, except as to the Places of chusing Senators.

The Congress shall assemble at least once in every Year, and such Meeting shall be on the first Monday in December, unless they shall by Law appoint a different Day.

AMENDMENT XIV

Rights Guaranteed: Privileges and Immunities of Citizenship, Due Process, and Equal Protection

Section 1

All persons born or naturalized in the United States, and subject to the jurisdiction thereof, are citizens of the United States and of the State wherein they reside. No State shall make or enforce any law which shall abridge the privileges or immunities of citizens of the United States; nor shall any State deprive any person of life, liberty, or property, without due process of law; nor deny to any person within its jurisdiction the equal protection of the laws.

AMENDMENT XV—RIGHTS OF CITIZENS TO VOTE

Section 1

The right of citizens of the United States to vote shall not be denied or abridged by the United States or by any State on account of race, color, or previous condition of servitude.

Section 2

The Congress shall have the power to enforce this article by appropriate legislation.

Document B

Online and Organizational Information Sources

1. Every state has a website that provides the basic information about its legislature. All you have to do is search online "State Legislature of [State Name]." For example, the Alabama State Legislature website provides links to: Legislation, Code & Constitution, Serrate Live Audio, House Live Audio, House Members, Senate Members, Profiled Bills, Joint Interim Committees, Legislative Process, House Rules, Senate Rules, Joint Rules, Legislative History, and Visitors Guide.

   Do the same for the constitution of your state, as well as the elections bureau, usually part of your state's department of state. Each state is different, but a good place to start for your state is the legislative website.

2. The best single source of information on legislatures from a national point of view is the NCSL (for National Conference of State Legislatures), 7700 East First Place, Denver, CO 80230. Telephone number: (303) 364-7700.

   NCSL is the trade association of the fifty state legislatures and is staffed by several dozen professional and knowledgeable individuals with considerable legislative experience. NCSL is continually studying state legislative issues and making available to the public the results of its studies. Go to www.ncsl.org.

   The NCSL has posted considerable information on congressional (and state legislative) redistricting. Go to "NCSL Redistricting Congress." You will find the redistricting criteria, the list of initiative and referendum states, and the states with commission-drawn congressional plans, as well as bills pending in each state, updates on court cases, and other information. The first three of these postings are printed in the toolbox as Documents D, E, and F.

The director of the NCSL section on redistricting is Wendy Underhill, who is quite knowledgeable on redistricting across the country.

3. The site with the most comprehensive information devoted exclusively to redistricting is probably "All About Redistricting," produced by Professor Justin Levitt of Loyola Law School in Los Angeles. Go to www.redistricting.lls.edu. The site has apparently complete reporting on redistricting in each state, the court cases, and updates on developments as they occur. Professor Levitt has written extensively on redistricting, and his publications are listed.

4. The Brennan Center for Justice at New York University focuses on seven issues, two of which are redistricting and money in politics. The Brennan Center developed the model for calculating the efficiency gap provided in this toolbox as Document H. Go online to the Brennan Center for Justice site, www.brennancenter.org.

5. On money in state politics, the best source is the National Institute on Money in State Politics, 833 North Last Chance Gulch, Helena, MT 59601. Telephone number: (406) 449-2480. This project operates the website www.followthemoney.org/ that is a comprehensive overview and state-by-state report on how money is spent to influence legislatures. Besides the segment it has devoted to independent expenditures discussed in chapter 3, the site has links that include: My District, Point of Influence, National Overview, Industry Influence, Timelines, and also a Deeper Focus on subjects like independent spending. This project also has the only source of amounts spent on lobbying in some states. Document G shows the institute's criteria for scoring Independent Expenditure reporting requirements.

6. The League of Women Voters is a national organization that advocates for reform of redistricting and money in politics. Through its state chapters the league has been instrumental in making redistricting reforms in states like Florida. The league's contact information is 1730 M Street NW, Suite 1000, Washington, DC 20036-4508. Telephone number: (202) 429-1965 and fax: (202) 429-0854. Wylecia Wiggs Harris is the CEO. The league's website is www.lwv.org.

7. Common Cause is a national organization with chapters in most states that seeks reform in redistricting and money in politics. Its website, www.commoncause.org, has a section on redistricting that shows state redistricting campaigns, litigation, an activist handbook, a gerrymandering gazette, and redistricting events. Kathay Feng, the executive director of the California chapter, is also the national redistricting director for Common Cause. Her email is kfeng@commoncause.org/, and her telephone is (213) 623-1216.

8. The Pew Center on the States is devoted to the idea that "good policy depends on good information." Its focus is on issues affecting state government generally, rather than on the legislatures themselves. It is located at 901 E Street NW, Washington, DC 20004-2008. Telephone number: (202) 552-2000. Its website is www.pewstates.org.

COMPUTER SOFTWARE PROGRAMS

Redistricting autoBound is a product of Citygate GIS and claims to be the most widely used redistricting system in North America (www.citygategis.com/products). If you have your own copy of ArcGIS, the software costs between $4,800 and $5,800.

Maptitude is a product of the Caliper Corporation and is also popular, www.caliper.com. Maptitude for Redistricting with one state of data is priced at $10,000. Maptitude is $695, and the redistricting data is available at 2,500 per state.

These programs can be expensive, but there are a number of sites that offer the experience of drawing districting lines on a basic level, but not with the same sophisitication that the professionals use with the expensive programs. Go to "drawing redistricting lines" on your computer browser.

The Brennan Center for Justice and the Committee of Seventy in Philadelphia offer a chance to draw district plans free of charge. The Redistricting 101 section of the Brennan Center site, described previously, has a segment How to Draw the Lines with a link to a step-by-step guide to draw district lines.

Document C

Bibliography and Suggestions for Further Reading

CONSTITUTIONAL BACKGROUND

Bowen, Catherine Drinker. *Miracle at Philadelphia: The Story of the Constitutional Convention May to September 1787*. Boston: Little, Brown and Company, 1966.

De Tocqueville, Alexis. *Democracy in America*. New York: Vintage Books, 1945.

Gutzman, Kevin R. C. *James Madison and the Making of America*. New York: St. Martin's Press, 2012.

Hamilton, Alexander, James Madison, and John Jay. *The Federalist. A Commentary on the Constitution of the United States*. New York: Tudor Publishing, 1947.

CONTEMPORARY

Daley, David. *Ratf**ked: The True Story Behind the Secret Plan to Steal American Democracy*. New York: Liveright, 2016.

Hofeller, Thomas, B. *What I've Learned about Redistricting the Hard Way*. PowerPoint presentation. National Conference of State Legislatures, January 24, 2011. http://www.ncsl.org/documents/legismgt/The_Hard_Way.pdf. (Hofeller is acknowledged as one of the outstanding practitioners of the map drawing art for the Republicans. This PowerPoint lecture offers great insight into how it is done.)

Kury, Franklin L. *Why Are You Here? A Primer for State Legislators and Citizens.* Lanham, MD: University Press of America, 2014.

Mayer, Jane. *Dark Money: The Hidden History of the Billionaires behind the Rise of the Radical Right.* New York: Anchor Books, 2016.

OTHER SOURCES OF INFORMATION AND HELP

Many colleges and universities have political science or government study programs that do work on redistricting. Check with your local college or university. The foregoing list of documents, books, organizations, and other sources of information are not intended to be conclusive or complete. There is a great deal available to the public, and I encourage the readers to use this toolbox to get started, but not necessarily to end with it.

Document D

Redistricting Criteria for Each State

This material is reproduced by permission from the National Conference of State Legislatures.

REDISTRICTING CRITERIA

When redistricting, state legislatures or redistricting commissions are provided certain criteria with which to draw the lines. These criteria are intended to make the districts easy to identify and understand, and to ensure fairness and consistency.

All states must comply with the federal constitutional requirements related to population and antidiscrimination. For congressional redistricting, the Apportionment Clause of Article I, Section 2, of the US Constitution requires that all districts be as nearly equal in population as practicable, which essentially means exactly equal. For state legislative districts, the Equal Protection Clause of the Fourteenth Amendment to the US Constitution requires that districts be substantially equal. Some say that 10 percent deviation in population from one district to the next is a safe standard. However, that has not proven to be a guaranteed protection from court scrutiny or revision. As such, several states have provided for their own deviation standard. For instance, Colorado prohibits districts from having a population deviation above 5 percent (Colo. Const. Art. V, § 46).

In addition to population equality, Section 2 of the Voting Rights Act of 1965 prohibits plans that intentionally or inadvertently discriminate on the basis of race, which could dilute the minority vote.

In addition to these mandatory standards set out by the US Constitution and the Voting Rights Act, states are allowed to adopt their own redistricting criteria, or principles, for drawing the plans.

These traditional districting principles (or criteria) have been adopted by many states:

- Compactness: Having the minimum distance between all the parts of a constituency (a circle, square, or a hexagon is the most compact district).
- Contiguity: All parts of a district being connected at some point with the rest of the district.
- Preservation of counties and other political subdivisions: This refers to not splitting counties up too much if possible or not crossing town, city, or county boundaries when drawing districts.
- Preservation of communities of interest: Geographical areas, such as neighborhoods of a city or regions of a state, where the residents have common political interests that do not necessarily coincide with the boundaries of a political subdivision, such as a city or county.
- Preservation of cores of prior districts: This refers to maintaining districts as previously drawn, to the extent possible. This leads to continuity of representation.
- Protection of incumbents: This requires the redistricting authority to ensure competitive districts by not concerning themselves with the address or residence of the incumbent. Or on the flip side, requiring the redistricting authority to take into account the address and residence of the incumbent to ensure that two incumbents are not opposing one another.

These emerging criteria have been considered and adopted in a few states since 2000:

- Competitiveness: Districts having relatively even partisan balance, making competition between the two major parties more intense. These criteria typically seek to avoid the creation of safe districts for a particular party. For instance, Arizona statute (cited below) states that "to the extent practicable, competitive districts should be favored where to do so would create no significant detriment to the other goals." This concept sometimes goes hand in hand with the traditional protection of incumbents criteria detailed above.

- Prohibition on using partisan data: Line drawers, whether they be commissioners (Arizona and California), nonpartisan staff (Iowa), or legislators (Florida) are prohibited from using partisan data as an input when redrawing districts, or for any other purpose in the re-districting process.

Table D.1. State Redistricting Criteria

State	Legislative or Congressional	Criteria	Citation
Alabama	Legislative	Required: Compact, Contiguous, Preserve political subdivisions, Preserve communities of interest Allowed: Protect incumbents	Ala. Const. Art. IX, §§ 198-200; Reapportionment Committee Guidelines
Alabama	Congressional	Required: Compact, Contiguous, Preserve political subdivisions, Preserve communities of interest Allowed: Protect incumbents	
Alaska	Legislative	Required: Compact, Contiguous, Preserve political subdivisions, Preserve communities of interest	Alaska Const. Art. VI
Alaska	Congressional	Only one congressional district	
Arizona	Legislative	Required: Compact, Contiguous, Preserve political subdivisions, Preserve communities of interest Prohibited: Protect incumbents, Use of partisan data	Ariz. Const. Art. 4, pt. 2, § 1; *Competitiveness
Arizona	Congressional	Required: Compact, Contiguous, Preserve political subdivisions, Preserve communities of interest Prohibited: Protect incumbents, Use of partisan data	
Arkansas	Legislative	Required: Preserve political subdivisions, Preserve cores of prior districts Allowed: Protect incumbents	Legislative: Ark. Const. Art. 8
Arkansas	Congressional	Required: Contiguous, Preserve political subdivisions, Preserve cores of prior districts Allowed: Protect incumbents	House Concurrent Resolution No. 1006, 1991 Session

State	Type	Requirements	Citation
California	Legislative	Required: Compact, Contiguous, Preserve political subdivisions, Preserve communities of interest; Prohibited: Protect incumbents, Use of partisan data	Cal. Const. Art. 21, §§ 1, 2;
California	Congressional	Required: Compact, Contiguous, Preserve political subdivisions, Preserve communities of interest; Prohibited: Protect incumbents, Use of partisan data	*Competitiveness
Colorado	Legislative	Required: Compact, Contiguous, Preserve political subdivisions, Preserve communities of interest	Colo. Const. Art. V, §§ 47
Colorado	Congressional	Required: Compact, Contiguous, Preserve political subdivisions, Preserve communities of interest	
Connecticut	Legislative	Required: Contiguous, Preserve political subdivisions	Conn. Const. Art. III, § 3, as amended by Article II, Section 1, and Article XV, Section 1, of the Amendments to the Constitution of the State of Connecticut;
Connecticut	Congressional	Required: Contiguous, Preserve political subdivisions	Conn. Const. Art. III, § 4, as amended by Article II, Section 2, and Article XV, Section 2, of the Amendments to the Constitution of the State of Connecticut; Conn. Const. Art. III, § 5, as amended by Article XVI, Section 1, of the Amendments to the Constitution of the State of Connecticut
Delaware	Legislative	Required: Contiguous; Prohibited: Protect incumbents	Del. Code tit. 29, § 804
Delaware	Congressional	Only one congressional district	

(continued)

Table D.1. *Continued*

State	Legislative or Congressional	Criteria	Citation
Florida	Legislative	Required: Compact, Contiguous, Preserve political subdivisions Prohibited: Protect incumbents, Use of partisan data (as interpreted by courts)	Fla. Const. Art. III, § 20 *Competitiveness
Florida	Congressional	Required: Compact, Contiguous, Preserve political subdivisions Prohibited: Protect incumbents, Use of partisan data (as interpreted by courts)	
Georgia	Legislative	Required: Compact, Contiguous, Preserve political subdivisions, Preserve communities of interest Allowed: Protect incumbents	Ga. Const. Art. III, § 2, Para. II
Georgia	Congressional	Required: Compact, Contiguous, Preserve political subdivisions, Preserve communities of interest Allowed: Protect incumbents	
Hawaii	Legislative	Required: Compact, Contiguous, Preserve political subdivisions, Preserve communities of interest Prohibited: Protect incumbents	Hawaii Const. Art. IV, § 6; Hawaii Rev. Stat. § 25-2(b)(1)to(6);
Hawaii	Congressional	Required: Compact, Contiguous, Preserve political subdivisions, Preserve communities of interest Prohibited: Protect incumbents	Competitiveness

State	Type	Requirements	Citation
Idaho	Legislative	Required: Contiguous, Preserve political subdivisions, Preserve communities of interest Prohibited: Protect incumbents	Idaho Const. Art. III, § 5; Idaho Code § 72-1506;
Idaho	Congressional	Required: Contiguous, Preserve political subdivisions, Preserve communities of interest Prohibited: Protect incumbents	
Illinois	Legislative Congressional	Required: Compact, Contiguous No additional requirements	Ill. Const. Art. IV, § 3
Indiana Illinois	Legislative Congressional	Required: Contiguous No additional requirements	Ind. Const. Art. 4, § 5
Iowa	Legislative	Required: Compact, Contiguous, Preserve political subdivisions Prohibited: Protect incumbents, Use of partisan data	Iowa Const. Art. III, §§ 34 & 37; Iowa Code § 42.4
Iowa	Congressional	Required: Compact, Contiguous, Preserve political subdivisions Prohibited: Protect incumbents, Use of partisan data	
Kansas	Legislative	Required: Compact, Contiguous, Preserve political subdivisions, Preserve communities of interest, Protect incumbents	Kan. Const. Art. 10, § 1 Kan. Stat. 4-101 et.seq.
Kansas	Congressional	Required: Compact, Contiguous, Preserve political subdivisions, Preserve communities of interest, Preserve cores of prior districts	Guidelines and Criteria for 2012 Kansas Congressional and Legislative Redistricting, Kansas Legislative Research Department, January 9, 2012
Kentucky Kentucky	Legislative Congressional	Required: Contiguous, Preserve political subdivisions Required: Contiguous, Preserve political subdivisions, Preserve communities of interest	Ky. Const. § 33

(continued)

Table D.1. Continued

State	Legislative or Congressional	Criteria	Citation
Louisiana	Legislative	Required: Contiguous, Preserve political subdivisions, Preserve cores of prior districts	LSA-Const. Art. 3, § 6 Title XVIII—Louisiana Election Code
Louisiana	Congressional	Required: Contiguous, Preserve political subdivisions, Preserve cores of prior districts	Committee Rules for Redistricting, Louisiana House of Representatives, Subcommittee on Reapportionment of the Committee on House and Governmental Affairs, January 19, 2011
			Committee Rules for Redistricting, Louisiana Senate, Committee on Senate and Governmental Affairs, February 16, 2011
Maine	Legislative	Required: Compact, Contiguous, Preserve political subdivisions	Me. Const. Art. IV, Part First, § 2; Me. Rev. Stat. tit. 21A, § 1206;
Maine	Congressional	Required: Compact, Contiguous, Preserve political subdivisions	Me. Rev. Stat. tit. 21A, § 1206-A
Maryland	Legislative	Required: Compact, Contiguous, Preserve political subdivisions	Md. Const. Art. III, § 4;
Maine	Congressional	No additional requirements	
Massachusetts	Legislative	Required: Contiguous, Preserve political subdivisions	Mass. Const. Art. Of Amend., art. Cl
Massachusetts	Congressional	No additional requirements	
Michigan	Legislative	Required: Compact, Contiguous, Preserve political subdivisions, Preserve cores of prior districts	Mich. Const. Art. IV, § 2; Mich. Comp. Laws § 3.63;
Michigan	Congressional	Required: Compact, Contiguous, Preserve political subdivisions	Mich. Comp. Laws § 4.261; Mich. Comp. Laws § 4.261a

State	Type	Requirements	Citation
Minnesota	Legislative	Required: Compact, Contiguous, Preserve political subdivisions, Preserve communities of interest	Minn. Const. Art. IV, §§ 2-3; Minn. Stat. § 2.91;
Minnesota	Congressional	Required: Compact, Contiguous, Preserve political subdivisions, Preserve communities of interest	Order Stating Redistricting Principles and Requirements for Plan Submissions, November 4, 2011.
Mississippi	Legislative	Required: Compact, Contiguous, Preserve political subdivisions	Miss. Code §5-3-101
Mississippi	Congressional	No additional requirements	
Missouri	Legislative	Required: Compact, Contiguous, Preserve political subdivisions	Mo. Const. Art. 3, § 2 Mo. Const. Art. 3, § 45
Missouri	Congressional	Required: Compact, Contiguous	
Montana	Legislative	Required: Compact, Contiguous, Preserve political subdivisions Prohibited: Protect incumbents	Mont. Const. Art. V, § 14 Mont. Code Ann. § 5-1-115
Montana	Congressional	Only one congressional district	
Nebraska	Legislative	Required: Compact, Contiguous, Preserve political subdivisions, Preserve cores of prior districts Prohibited: Protect incumbents	Neb. Const. Art. III, § 5; Legislative Resolution No. 7, adopted by the Nebraska Legislature, 2001
Nebraska	Congressional	Required: Compact, Contiguous, Preserve political subdivisions, Preserve cores of prior districts Prohibited: Protect incumbents	
Nevada	Legislative	Required: Compact, Contiguous, Preserve political subdivisions, Preserve communities of interest, Preserve cores of prior districts, Protect incumbents	N.R.S. Const. Art. 13, § 15 N.R.S. Ch. 304, App.
Nevada	Congressional	Required: Compact, Contiguous, Preserve political subdivisions, Preserve communities of interest, Preserve cores of prior districts, Protect incumbents	Assembly Concurrent Resolution No. 1, Joint Standing Rules, adopted February 12, 2001, Rules 13.1, 13.3, 13.5

Table D.1. *Continued*

State	Legislative or Congressional	Criteria	Citation
New Hampshire	Legislative	Required: Contiguous, Preserve political subdivisions	N.H. Const., Part Second, House of Representatives, Art. 9, 11, 11-a;
New Hampshire	Congressional	No additional requirements	N.H. Const., Part Second, Senate, Art. 26
New Jersey	Legislative	Required: Compact, Contiguous, Preserve political subdivisions	N.J. Const. Art. IV, § 2
New Jersey	Congressional	No additional requirements	
New Mexico	Legislative	Required: Compact, Contiguous, Preserve political subdivisions, Preserve communities of interest Allowed: Preserve cores of prior districts, Protect incumbents	N.M. Stat. Ann. § 2-7C-3; N.M. Stat. Ann. § 2-8D-2; Guidelines for the Development of State and Congressional Redistricting Plans
New Mexico	Congressional	Required: Compact, Contiguous, Preserve political subdivisions, Preserve communities of interest Allowed: Preserve cores of prior districts, Protect incumbents	
New York	Legislative	Required: Compact, Contiguous, Preserve political subdivisions	N.Y. Const. Art. III, § 4 & 5
New York	Congressional	Required: Compact, Contiguous, Preserve cores of prior districts Prohibited: Protect incumbents	*Competitiveness: new commission
North Carolina	Legislative	Required: Contiguous, Preserve political subdivisions, Preserve communities of interest, Preserve political subdivisions	N.C. Const. Art. II, §§ 3 & 5;
North Carolina	Congressional	Required: Contiguous, Preserve political subdivisions	Overview of Redistricting Process, N.C. General Assembly
North Dakota	Legislative	Required: Compact, Contiguous	N.D. Const. Art. IV, § 2;
North Dakota	Congressional	Only one congressional district	N.D. Cent. Code § 54-03-01.5;

Ohio	Legislative	Required: Compact, Contiguous, Preserve political subdivisions	Ohio Const. Art. XI, §§ 3, 6, 7, 9, 10, 11
Ohio	Congressional	Required: Compact, Contiguous, Preserve political subdivisions	
Oklahoma	Legislative	Required: Compact, Contiguous, Preserve political subdivisions, Preserve communities of interest	Okla. Const. Art. 5, § 9A
Oklahoma	Congressional	No additional requirements	
Oregon	Legislative	Required: Contiguous, Preserve political subdivisions, Preserve communities of interest Prohibited: Protect incumbents	Legislative Guide to Redistricting, 2011 Or. Const. Art. IV, § 7; Or. Rev. Stat. § 188.010
Oregon	Congressional	Required: Contiguous, Preserve political subdivisions, Preserve communities of interest Prohibited: Protect incumbents	
Pennsylvania	Legislative	Required: Compact, Contiguous, Preserve political subdivisions	Penn. Const. Art. II, § 16
Pennsylvania	Congressional	No additional requirements	
Rhode Island	Legislative	Required: Compact, Contiguous, Preserve political subdivisions	R.I. Const. Art. VII, § 1; R.I. Const. Art. VIII, § 1
Rhode Island	Congressional	Required: Compact, Contiguous, Preserve political subdivisions	2011 R.I. Laws ch. 106, § 1; 2011 R.I. Laws ch. 100, § 1
South Carolina	Legislative	Required: Compact, Contiguous, Preserve political subdivisions, Preserve communities of interest, Preserve cores of prior districts Allowed: Protect incumbents	Guidelines for Legislative and Congressional Redistricting, adopted April 13, 2011
South Carolina	Congressional	Required: Compact, Contiguous, Preserve political subdivisions, Preserve communities of interest, Preserve cores of prior districts Allowed: Protect incumbents	

(continued)

Table D.1. *Continued*

State	Legislative or Congressional	Criteria	Citation
South Dakota	Legislative	Required: Compact, Contiguous, Preserve political subdivisions, Preserve communities of interest	S.D. Const. Art. III, § 5; S.D. Codified Laws § 2-2-41
South Dakota	Congressional	Only one congressional district	
Tennessee	Legislative	Required: Contiguous, Preserve political subdivisions	Tenn. Code § 3-1-102; Tenn. Code § 3-1-103
Tennessee	Congressional	No additional requirements	
Texas	Legislative	Required: Contiguous, Preserve political subdivisions	Tex. Const. Art. III, §§ 25 & 26
Texas	Congressional	No additional requirements	
Utah	Legislative	Required: Compact, Contiguous	U.C.A. 1953, Const. Art. 9, § 1
Utah	Congressional	Required: Compact, Contiguous	
Vermont	Legislative	Required: Compact, Contiguous, Preserve political subdivisions, Preserve communities of interest Allowed: Protect incumbents	2011 Redistricting Principles, adopted by the Legislative Redistricting Committee, May 2011 Vt. Const. Ch. II, §§ 13 & 18; Vt. Stat. Ann. tit. 17, ch. 34A, §§ 1903, 1906b, 1906c
Vermont	Congressional	Only one congressional district	
Virginia	Legislative	Required: Compact, Contiguous, Preserve communities of interest	Va. Const. Art. II, § 6; Va. Code § 24.2-305;
Virginia	Congressional	Required: Compact, Contiguous, Preserve communities of interest	Redistricting Criteria, Division of Legislative Services

State	Type	Requirements	Citation
Washington	Legislative	Required: Compact, Contiguous, Preserve political subdivisions, Preserve communities of interest Prohibited: Protect incumbents	Wash. Const., Art. II, § 43; Wash. Rev. Code § 44.05.090
Washington	Congressional	Required: Compact, Contiguous, Preserve political subdivisions, Preserve communities of interest Prohibited: Protect incumbents	
West Virginia	Legislative	Required: Compact, Contiguous, Preserve political subdivisions	W. Va. Const., Art. I, § 4; W. Va. Const., Art. VI, § 4
West Virginia	Congressional	Required: Compact, Contiguous	
Wisconsin	Legislative	Required: Compact, Contiguous, Preserve political subdivisions	Wis. Const., Art. IV, §§ 3-5;
Wisconsin	Congressional	No additional requirements	
Wyoming	Legislative	Required: Compact, Contiguous, Preserve political subdivisions, Preserve communities of interest	Wyo. Const. Art. 3, § 49;
Wyoming	Congressional	Required: Compact, Contiguous, Preserve political subdivisions Note: Only one congressional district	Redistricting Principles—2011, Joint Corporations, Elections and Political Subdivisions Interim Committee, April 2011

Source: National Conference of State Legislatures, "Redistricting Criteria for Each State," June 27, 2017.

Document E

Initiative and Referendum States

This material is reproduced by permission from the National Conference of State Legislatures.

Initiative—a law or constitutional amendment introduced by citizens through a petition process either to the legislature or directly to the voters.

Popular referendum—a process by which voters may petition to demand a popular vote on a new law passed by the legislature.

Table E.1. Initiative and Referendum States

| State | Statutes | | Constitution |
	Initiative	Popular Referendum	Initiative
Alaska	I*	Yes	None
Arizona	D	Yes	D
Arkansas	D	Yes	D
California	D	Yes	D
Colorado	D	Yes	D
Florida	None	No	D
Idaho	D	Yes	None
Illinois	None	No	D
Maine	I	Yes	None
Maryland	None	Yes	None
Massachusetts	I	Yes	I
Michigan	I	Yes	D
Mississippi	None	No	I
Missouri	D	Yes	D
Montana	D	Yes	D
Nebraska	D	Yes	D
Nevada	I	Yes	D
New Mexico	None	Yes	None
North Dakota	D	Yes	D
Ohio	I	Yes	D
Oklahoma	D	Yes	D
Oregon	D	Yes	D
South Dakota	D	Yes	D
Utah	D & I	Yes	None
Washington	D & I	Yes	None
Wyoming	I*	Yes	None
U.S. Virgin Islands	I	Yes	I

Note: D = *direct initiative*, proposals that qualify go directly on the ballot; I = *indirect initiative*, proposals are submitted to the legislature, which has an opportunity to act on the proposed legislation. The initiative question will subsequently go on the ballot if the legislature rejects it, submits a different proposal, or takes no action.
*Alaska and Wyoming's initiative processes are usually considered indirect. However, instead of requiring that an initiative be submitted to the legislature for action, they only require that an initiative cannot be placed on the ballot until after a legislative session has convened and adjourned.

Source: National Conference of State Legislatures, "Initiative and Referendum States," December 2015, http://www.ncsl.org/research/elections-and-campaigns/chart-of-the-initiative-states.aspx.

Document F

Redistricting Commissions: Congressional Plans

This material is reproduced by permission from the National Conference of State Legislatures.

REDISTRICTING COMMISSIONS: CONGRESSIONAL PLANS

Traditionally, state legislatures have been responsible for redistricting for state legislative and congressional districts. Since the landmark Supreme Court decisions of the 1960s that established the one-person, one-vote principle, a number of states have shifted redistricting of state legislative district lines from the legislature to a board or commission. There are pros and cons to removing the process from the traditional legislative process to a commission. Reformers often mistakenly assume that commissions will be less partisan than legislatures when conducting redistricting but that depends largely on the design of the board or commission.

NCSL has categorized the commissions as either having primary responsibility for redistricting, serving in an advisory capacity, or operating as a backup commission in cases where the legislature does not meet its deadline. All states not represented in the tables below draw congressional districts through state legislative authority.

Six states have a commission with primary responsibility for drawing a plan for congressional districts. Five states have an advisory commission that may assist the legislature with drawing the district lines and two states have a backup commission that will make the decision if the legislature is unable to agree. Also see below for Iowa's redistricting plan, which is distinct from the other categories.

Also check out NCSL's Redistricting Commissions: State Legislative Plans webpage for more on how commission states use commissions to draw state legislative district lines, and NCSL's Redistricting Commission Bills for 2017 legislation.

Table F.1. Commissions with Primary Responsibility for Drawing a Plan for Congressional Districts

State	Number of Members	Details
Arizona Ariz. Const. art. IV, pt. 2, § 1	5	Name: Independent Redistricting Commission Selection requirements: The commission on appellate court appointees creates a pool of twenty-five nominees, ten from each of the two largest parties and five not from either of the two largest parties. The highest ranking officer of the house appoints one from the pool, then the minority leader of the house appoints one, then the highest ranking officer of the senate appoints one, then the minority leader of the senate appoints one. These four appoint a fifth from the pool, not a member of any party already represented on the commission, as chair. If the four deadlock, the commission on appellate court appointments appoints the chair.
California Cal. Const. Article XXI	14	Name: Citizen's Redistricting Commission Selection requirements: With the passage of Proposition 11 in 2008, the process of redrawing California's congressional districts was removed from state legislative authority and given to a newly established fourteen-member commission. The commission must include five Democrats, five Republicans, and four members from neither party. Government auditors are to select sixty registered voters from an applicant pool. Legislative leaders can reduce the pool; the auditors then are to pick eight commission members by lottery, and those commissioners pick six additional members for fourteen total. For approval district boundaries need votes from three Democratic commissioners, three Republican commissioners, and three commissioners from neither party.
Hawaii Hawaii Const. art. IV	9	Name: Reapportionment Commission Selection requirements: President of the senate selects two. Speaker of the house selects two. The minority leader in both the house and senate party each select one of their members. Those two each select one. These eight select the ninth member, who is the chair. No commission member may run for the legislature in the two elections following redistricting.

(continued)

Table F.1. *Continued*

State	Number of Members	Details
Idaho Idaho Const. art. III, § 2	6	Name: Commission for Reapportionment Selection requirements: Leaders of two of the largest political parties in each house of the legislature each designate one member; chairs of the two parties whose candidates for governor received the most votes in the last election each designate one member. No member may be an elected or appointed official in the state at the time of designation.
Montana* Mont. Const. art. V, § 14	5	Name: Commission Selection requirements: Majority and minority leaders of both houses of the legislature each select one member. Those four select a fifth, who is the chair. Members cannot be public officials. Members cannot run for public office in the two years after the completion of redistricting.
New Jersey N.J. Const. art. II, § II	13	Apportionment Commission Selection requirements: The majority and minority leaders in each legislative chamber and the chairs of the state's two major political parties each choose two commissioners, none of whom may be a congressional member or employee. Those twelve commissioners then choose a thirteenth who has not held any public or party office in New Jersey within the last five years. If the twelve commissioners are not able to select a thirteenth member to serve as chair, they will present two names to the state Supreme Court, which will choose the chair.
Washington Wash. Const. art. II, § 43	5	Name: Commission Selection requirements: The majority and minority party leaders in each legislative chamber each select one registered voter to serve as commissioner, and those four commissioners choose a nonvoting fifth commissioner to serve as chair.

Note: *Montana currently has just one congressional district, so the commission is not used.

Source: National Conference of State Legislatures, "Redistricting Congressional Plans," December 8, 2015, http://www.ncsl.org/research/redistricting/redistricting-commissions-congressional-plans.aspx.

Table F.2. Advisory Commissions

State	Number of Members	Details
Maine Me. Const. art. IV, pt. 3, § 1-A Me. Rev. Stat. tit. 21-A, § 1206	15	Name: Apportionment Commission Selection requirements: Speaker of the house appoints three. House minority leader appoints three. President of the senate appoints two. Senate minority leader appoints two. Chairs of two major political parties each choose one. The members from the two parties represented on the commission each appoint a public member, and the two public members choose a third public member.
New York (This commission was established to begin in the 2020 cycle, by a 2014 referendum, Proposal 1.)	10	Name: Independent Redistricting Commission Selection requirements: Each of the four legislative leaders appoints two members; the original eight members select two additional members. Legislators and other elected officials are prohibited from serving. If plans submitted by the commission are rejected by the legislature twice, the legislature will amend it as necessary.
Ohio Ohio Rev. Code § 103.51	6	Name: Legislative Task Force on Redistricting, Reapportionment, and Demographic Research Selection requirements: The majority leaders from both legislative chambers each appoint three members, at least one of whom must be from a different party, and at least one of whom is not a legislator.
Rhode Island 2011 R.I. Laws ch. 106, § 1 2011 R.I. Laws ch. 100, § 1	18	Name: Reapportionment Commission Selection requirements: The majority leader of both the house and the senate chose four members of the legislature and three who are not. The senate and house minority leaders each choose two who are not members of the legislature.
Virginia Exec. Order No. 31 (2011)	11	Name: Independent Bipartisan Advisory Commission on Redistricting Selection requirements: Governor created an advisory commission in 2011 by executive order. The commission is designed to get public input and to recommend district lines to the legislature, which may adopt, modify, or ignore the commission's proposals. Governor chooses five citizens of each majority party who have not held elected office in the last five years and are not employees of Congress or the state legislature. Governor will also select the chair, who is not identifiable with any political party.

Note: *Montana currently has just one congressional district, so the commission is not used.

Source: National Conference of State Legislatures, "Redistricting Congressional Plans," December 8, 2015, http://www.ncsl.org/research/redistricting/redistricting-commissions-congressional-plans.aspx.

Table F.3. Backup Commissions

State	Number of Members	Details

Connecticut
Conn. Const.
  art. III, § 6,
  amend.
  XXVI(b)
	9	Name: Commission
		Selection requirements: President pro tem of the senate, senate minority leader, speaker of the house, and house minority leader each select two; these eight must select the ninth within thirty days.

Indiana Ind. Code § 3-3-2-2	5	Name: Redistricting Commission Selection requirements: The commission is made up of the speaker of the house, president pro tem of the senate, the chair of the redistricting committee from each legislative chamber, and a state legislator nominated by the governor.

Note: *Montana currently has just one congressional district, so the commission is not used.

Source: National Conference of State Legislatures, "Redistricting Congressional Plans," December 8, 2015, http://www.ncsl.org/research/redistricting/redistricting-commissions-congressional-plans.aspx.

Table F.4. Other

Iowa	Iowa conducts redistricting unlike any other state. The Iowa system does not put the task in the hands of a commission, but rather the legislature does vote on the plans. Nonpartisan legislative staff develop maps for the Iowa House and Senate as well as US House districts without any political or election data including the addresses of incumbents. This is different from all other states.

Note: *Montana currently has just one congressional district, so the commission is not used.

Source: National Conference of State Legislatures, "Redistricting Congressional Plans," December 8, 2015, http://www.ncsl.org/research/redistricting/redistricting-commissions-congressional-plans.aspx.

Document G

Criteria for Scoring Each State on Independent Expenditure Reporting Requirements

This material is reproduced by permission from the National Institute on Money in State Politics.

Table G.1.

State	Overall Score (max 120)	IE Disclosure (max 30)	IE Targets (max 10)	IE Positions (max 10)	EC Disclosure (max 30)	EC Targets (max 10)	EC Positions (max 10)	Donor Disclosure (max 20)
Alabama	0	0	0	0	0	0	0	0
Alaska	120	30	10	10	30	10	10	20
Arizona	110	30	10	10	30	10	10	10
Arkansas	40	30	0	0	0	0	0	10
California	110	30	10	10	30	10	0	20
Colorado	120	30	10	10	30	10	10	20
Connecticut	120	30	10	10	30	10	10	20
Delaware	120	30	10	10	30	10	10	20
Florida	100	30	5	5	30	5	5	20
Georgia	25	15	0	0	0	0	0	10
Hawaii	120	30	10	10	30	10	10	20
Idaho	120	30	10	10	30	10	10	20
Illinois	120	30	10	10	30	10	10	20
Indiana	0	0	0	0	0	0	0	0
Iowa	50	15	5	5	15	0	0	10
Kansas	110	30	10	5	30	10	5	20
Kentucky	60	30	10	10	0	0	0	10
Louisiana	60	30	10	10	0	0	0	10
Maine	120	30	10	10	30	10	10	20
Maryland	110	30	10	10	30	10	0	20
Massachusetts	110	30	10	10	30	10	0	20
Michigan	60	30	10	10	0	0	0	10
Minnesota	60	30	10	10	0	0	0	10
Mississippi	60	30	10	10	0	0	0	10
Missouri	60	30	10	10	0	0	0	10
Montana	110	30	10	5	30	10	5	20

State						
Nebraska	55	30	10	5	0	0	10
Nevada	80	30	0	0	30	0	20
New Hampshire	85	30	10	10	15	5	10
New Jersey	40	30	0	0	0	0	10
New Mexico	0	0	0	0	0	0	0
New York	70	30	10	0	15	5	10
North Carolina	110	30	10	10	30	10	20
North Dakota	70	15	5	5	15	5	20
Ohio	100	30	10	10	30	10	10
Oklahoma	100	30	10	10	30	10	10
Oregon	110	30	10	10	30	10	10
Pennsylvania	25	15	5	5	0	0	0
Rhode Island	120	30	10	10	30	10	20
South Carolina	0	0	0	0	0	0	0
South Dakota	50	15	5	0	15	5	10
Tennessee	35	15	5	5	0	0	10
Texas	120	30	10	10	30	10	20
Utah	120	30	10	10	30	10	20
Vermont	40	0	0	0	30	0	0
Virginia	60	30	10	10	0	0	10
Washington	110	30	10	10	30	10	10
West Virginia	100	30	10	0	30	10	20
Wisconsin	35	15	5	5	0	0	10
Wyoming	50	30	10	0	0	0	10

Note: IE = independent expenditures; EC = electioneering communications.

Source: Pete Quist, "Table 1: State Scorecard of Essential Independent Spending Disclosure Requirements," in *Scorecard: Essential Disclosure Requirements for Independent Spending, 2014*, National Institute on Money in State Politics, December 3, 2014, https://www.followthemoney.org/research/institute-reports/scorecard-essential-disclosure-requirements-for-independent-spending-2014.

Document H

How the Efficiency Gap Works

Eric Petry

This material is reproduced with permission from the Brennan Center for Justice.

HOW THE EFFICIENCY GAP WORKS

The efficiency gap is a standard for measuring partisan gerrymandering that is currently at the heart of the Wisconsin gerrymandering case, *Whitford v. Nichol.*[1]

Developed by Nicholas Stephanopoulos, professor at the University of Chicago Law School, and Eric McGhee, research fellow at the Public Policy Institute of California, the efficiency gap counts the number of votes each party wastes in an election to determine whether either party enjoyed a systematic advantage in turning votes into seats.[2] Any vote cast for a losing candidate is considered wasted, as are all the votes cast for a winning candidate in excess of the number needed to win.

Hypothetical Scenario

To understand how the efficiency gap works, consider a hypothetical state with 500 residents that is divided into five legislative districts, each with 100 voters. In the most recent election cycle, Democrats won districts 1 and 2 by wide margins, while Republicans won districts 3, 4, and 5 in closer races. Overall, Democratic candidates received 55 percent of the statewide vote but won just 40 percent of the legislative seats, while Republican candidates received 45 percent and won 60 percent of the seats. The table below shows the election results for each district.

Table H.1.

District	D Votes	R Votes	Result
1	75	25	D wins
2	60	40	D wins
3	43	57	R wins
4	48	52	R wins
5	49	51	R wins
Total	275	225	

Calculating the Efficiency Gap

Calculating the efficiency gap involves three steps.

Step 1: The first step is to determine the total number of votes each party wasted in the election. Again, any votes cast for a losing candidate are considered wasted. Likewise, any vote cast for a winning candidate in excess of the number needed to win is also wasted. In our scenario, a candidate needs fifty-one votes to win since there are 100 voters in each district, so any votes above that threshold are wasted. The table below shows the election results in each district, as well as the number of wasted votes.

Table H.2.

District	D Votes	R Votes	D Wasted Votes	R Wasted Votes	Net Wasted Votes
1	75	25	24	25	1 R
2	60	40	9	40	31 R
3	43	57	43	6	37 D
4	48	52	48	1	47 D
5	49	51	49	0	49 D
Total	275	225	173	72	101 D

Since the Democratic candidate in district 1 received seventy-five votes but only needed fifty to win, twenty-four Democratic votes were wasted (75 − 51 = 24). Likewise, all twenty-five Republican votes in district 1 were wasted since the Republican candidate lost.

Repeating this process for the other districts shows that in district 2 Democrats wasted nine votes and Republicans wasted forty votes, in district 3 Democrats wasted forty-three votes and Republicans wasted six votes, in district 4 Democrats wasted forty-eight votes and Republicans wasted one vote, and in district 5 Democrats wasted forty-nine votes and Republicans wasted zero votes.

Step 2: Next, the process requires calculating the total number of votes wasted by each party and finding the net wasted votes. In this scenario, Democrats wasted 173 votes $(24 + 9 + 43 + 48 + 49 = 173)$ and Republicans wasted 72 votes $(25 + 40 + 6 + 1 + 0 = 72)$. Thus, Democrats had a net waste of 101 votes $(173 - 72 = 101)$, meaning they wasted 101 more votes than Republicans.

Step 3: The final step in calculating the efficiency gap is to divide the net wasted votes by the total number of votes cast in the election. The net number of wasted votes was 101 and there were 500 total votes, which produces an efficiency gap of 20 percent $(101 \div 500 = .202)$.

In other words, Republicans were better able to convert their votes into legislative seats. As a result, they won 20 percent more seats (which translates to one additional seat since 20 percent of five equals one) than they would have if both parties had wasted an equal number of votes.

In their paper, Stephanopoulos and McGhee propose efficiency gap thresholds above which a district plan would be presumptively unconstitutional. For congressional plans, an efficiency gap of two or more seats indicates a constitutional problem. For state legislative plans, the threshold is an efficiency gap of 8 percent or greater.

Efficiency Gap Equation
    As an equation, the efficiency gap looks like this:

Efficiency gap = (Total Democratic wasted votes –
Total Republican wasted votes) ÷ Total votes

Simplified Efficiency Gap Calculation
    If either party's seat margin and vote margin for a given election are known, then the efficiency gap can also be calculated using the following formula:

Efficiency gap = (Seat margin – 50%) – 2 (Vote margin – 50%)

Applying this formula to the hypothetical yields the following algebraic process:

Efficiency gap = (Republican seat margin – 50%) –
2 (Republican vote margin – 50%)
Efficiency gap = (60% – 50%) – 2 (45% – 50%)
Efficiency gap = (10%) – 2 (–5%)
Efficiency gap = (10%) – (–10%)
Efficiency gap = 20%

Alternatively, using the Democratic seat and vote margins, the formula yields:

Efficiency gap = (Democratic seat margin – 50%) –
2 (Democratic vote margin – 50%)
Efficiency gap = (40% – 50%) – 2 (55% – 50%)
Efficiency gap = (–10%) – 2 (5%)
Efficiency gap = (–10%) – (10%)
Efficiency gap = –20%

When calculated using the margins for Republicans, who were better able to turn votes into seats, the efficiency gap is positive, indicating an electoral advantage. The converse is true when using the Democratic margins.

The simplified method for calculating the efficiency gap can be much faster than the district-by-district method, but note that the results are only exactly equal when voter turnout is equal in every district, as it is in this hypothetical.

NOTES

1. Whitford v. Nichol, No. 15-cv-421 (W.D. Wis. Filed July 8, 2015).
2. Nicholas O. Stephanopoulos and Eric M. McGee, *Partisan Gerrymandering and the Efficiency Gap*, 82 U. ChI. L. REV. 831 (2015).

Acknowledgments

I want to express my appreciation to a good number of folks who generously contributed their knowledge and critical judgment to this book. A work on a subject as complex as congressional redistricting would not be possible without such help and I was fortunate to receive it.

Wendy Underhill, program director for elections and redistricting for the National Conference of State Legislatures; Denise Roth Barber and Pete Quist of the National Institute on Money in State Politics; Thomas Wolf and Jessica Katzen of the Brennan Center for Justice; David Thornburgh of Committee of Seventy in Philadelphia.

On particular states, I was greatly aided by Christina Shupe, director of the California Citizens Redistricting Commission and Kathay Feng, executive director of the California Common Cause. Pamela Goodman, president of the League of Women Voters of Florida, and Carrie Davis, executive director of the League of Women Voters of Ohio, were most helpful on their states.

On Pennsylvania, I drew on my own experience in the state house and senate, but augmented it with input from Mark McKillop, former staff director on redistricting for the Senate Democrats; Drew Crompton, chief of staff to the senate president and general counsel to the majority caucus; Brent McClintock, executive director of the Pennsylvania Legislative Data Processing Center; Erik Arneson, aide to then Senate Majority Leader, Dominic Pileggi; former Republican Senator Robert Jubelirer; Senator Jay Costa, Democratic Floor Leader; Carol Kuniholm, leader of Fair Districts Pennsylvania; and C. J. Hafner, Counsel to the

Senate Democrats and Andrew S. Sislo, former Counsel to Pennsylvania's Department of State.

Colleagues and friends from my legislative days gave candid and helpful critiques: Vincent P. Carocci, Michael Aumiller, Joseph R. Powers, Neil McAulliffe, Paul Dlugolecki, and Michael McCarthy. William and Susan Ecenbarger provided insights from their experience in writing and publishing.

Three special individuals deserve thanks. Micheline Leininger, my typist, demonstrated her mastery of Word processing in readying the manuscript for publication.

JoHanna Wallner, my very capable editor.

My wife, Elizabeth, who was an editor of the *University of Pittsburgh Law Review*, gave unstintingly of her editorial skills and critical judgment.

To all of them, I say thank you!

Index

About the Author

PennLive/Harrisburg Patriot Media Group photo.

Franklin L. Kury is a former state legislator and attorney for whom this is his third book. The first book, *Clean Politics, Clean Streams*, an autobiography of his legislative career, was cited significantly by the Pennsylvania Supreme Court in a landmark case interpreting the environmental amendment to Pennsylvania's Constitution that he originated while a state representative. The second book, *Why Are You Here?*, is a primer for legislators and the public on state legislatures.

Kury served in the Pennsylvania House of Representatives and the State Senate. He is a graduate of Trinity College and the University of Pennsylvania Law School.

His website is: www.franklinkury.com.